countdown
CALENDARS

24 Stitched Projects to Celebrate Any Date

Compiled by Susanne Woods

stashBOOKS®

an imprint of C&T Publishing

Text, Photography, and Artwork copyright © 2011 by C&T Publishing

Publisher: Amy Marson

Creative Director: Gailen Runge

Acquisitions Editor: Susanne Woods

Editor: Lynn Koolish

Technical Editors: Sandy Peterson and Amanda Siegfried

Cover/Book Designer: Kristy Zacharias

Production Coordinator: Jessica Jenkins

Production Editor: Alice Mace Nakanishi

Illustrator: Kirstie Pettersen

Photography by Christina Carty-Francis and Diane Pedersen of C&T Publishing, Inc., unless otherwise noted

Published by Stash Books, an imprint of C&T Publishing, Inc., P.O. Box 1456, Lafayette, CA 94549

Library of Congress Cataloging-in-Publication Data

Countdown calendars : 24 stitched projects to celebrate any date / compiled by Susanne Woods.

p. cm.

ISBN 978-1-60705-174-9 (soft cover)

1. Textile crafts. 2. Sewing. 3. Holiday decorations. 4. Calendar. I. Woods, Susanne. II. C & T Publishing.

TT699.C685 2011

745.594'1--dc22

2010049072

Printed in China

10 9 8 7 6 5 4 3 2 1

Contents

Introduction

If patience is a virtue, my kids don't have it. My five and three-year-old boys are constantly anticipating exciting family events or holidays with regular inquiries as to how many days they have to wait until Thanksgiving, their birthdays, or our annual trip to the beach house. And who can blame them? The adult version may be crossing days off the calendar, but the truth is that we all love to look forward to these celebrations. What better way to focus this anticipation than with a countdown calendar? Countdown calendars somehow make the wait more bearable and make the ultimate event seem even more ... eventful. As with many of the ideas behind our Design Collective titles, this book saw its beginnings as I began to search around for a calendar for our family and was disappointed with what I found in the stores. As the acquisitions editor for Stash Books, I felt sure that I could find a group of inspirational, original alternatives to store-bought calendars that encourage you to create unique and personal projects instead.

This is the third book in our series of Design Collective titles, in which I have invited a variety of artists to share their fabulous creations with you. Within these pages you will find countdown calendars for a variety of holidays and events, but what I love most about them is that they can each be easily customized and personalized based on the fabric choices alone. Throughout, I have offered suggestions for different themes, objects to include in the pockets, and tips on how to make the projects even easier. Some of the projects are easily achievable, and some are a bit more of a challenge, but all are enjoyable, original, and artful designs. I hope you enjoy making and gifting these calendars for yourself, friends, and family.

—Susanne Woods

Back to School

Finished size: 8½˝ × 12˝

Whether returning to school after the winter break or starting a new year in the fall, this countdown calendar will keep everyone on track. Made from wool felt and embellished with embroidery, these miniature squares that mimic iconic staples of the classroom are secured with hook-and-loop tape to the ubiquitous lined-paper background. Use up your small scraps of felt, keep your eyes on your own "paper," and get to work on this handy reminder.

Amy Adams is a UK-based textile artist specializing in designing and making softies from an ever-increasing catalog of patterns. These softies are available as one-off pieces and as published patterns. Her work mixes vintage and recycled fabrics, as well as felted wool, with a dash of hand-stitched embroidery.

EMAIL:
lucykatecrafts@talktalk.net

WEBSITES:
lucykatecrafts.etsy.com
lucykatecrafts.co.uk
lucykatecrafts.blogspot.com

ARTIST: Amy Adams

MATERIALS AND CUTTING

Appliqué patterns are on page 99.

2 pieces 8½˝ × 12˝ cream or white craft felt for calendar base and backing

12 pieces 1½˝ × 1½˝ cream or white craft felt for calendar squares

1 piece 2˝ × 8˝ red craft felt for apple, book, and numbers 0, 2, and 4

1 piece 2˝ × 6˝ blue craft felt for globe, pencil, and numbers 1 and 5

1 piece 2˝ × 3˝ green craft felt for globe, apple leaf, and number 3

1 piece 2˝ × 4˝ brown craft felt for chalkboard, globe base, and apple stem

1 piece 2˝ × 2˝ tan craft felt for ruler

1 piece 2˝ × 2˝ black craft felt for chalkboard

1 piece 2˝ × 2˝ cream or white craft felt for book pages

1 piece 8½˝ × 11½˝ lightweight iron-on interfacing

1 length ¾˝ × 4½˝ cream or white sew-on hook-and-loop tape (just hooked side) for attaching calendar squares

1 piece 4˝ long of narrow ribbon for loop to hang calendar

Red and blue sewing thread

tip

This is a quick and easy project on a sewing machine. If you are not a sewer, the felt shapes can be glued in place to the calendar squares using fabric glue.

CONSTRUCTION

Calendar Base

1. Center the iron-on interfacing, glue side down, on the back side of the craft felt calendar base. Follow the manufacturer's directions to press and attach the interfacing to the craft felt.

2. Turn the calendar base faceup, and stitch all the blue horizontal lines to simulate notebook paper, starting 1˝ down from the top edge. Backstitch at the beginning and end of each line to secure the stitching. The stitched lines are ⅜˝ apart.

3. Stitch the red margin line 1¼˝ in from the left-hand edge.

Calendar Squares

1. Using the patterns (page 99), cut out the appliqué shapes from the colored craft felt.

2. Using the photographs (pages 6 and 9) as a guide, appliqué each number and motif to a 1½˝ × 1½˝ white or cream felt square using free-motion stitching (see Note, page 9). Add details as you stitch.

> ## tip
>
> Don't pin the appliqué pieces before stitching—some are just too small, and the pins will get in the way. The felt is fuzzy, and everything tends to stay in place on its own. The stitching will be easiest if you drop the feed dogs and free-motion stitch.

3. Trim all the loose threads, and pair up the squares as follows:

0 with the chalkboard

1 with the apple

2 with the pencil

3 with the book

4 with the ruler

5 with the globe

Place each pair wrong sides together, and, with the sewing machine set on a normal straight stitch, stitch around all 4 sides, slightly in from each edge.

Embroidery

1. Set the sewing machine for free-motion stitching, and stitch the title at the top of the front of the calendar base with the words, "How long 'til school starts?"

2. Count out the spacing (referring to the spaces between the blue horizontal lines rather than the lines themselves), and mark the third space down (counting the top space as 1) with a pin in the margin. Below this, mark the fifth space down, also with a pin in the margin. Continue marking every fifth space down until there are 6 pins in place. Each pin marks the space where a line of wording will be stitched.

3. Embroider each marked space with one of the following:

SCHOOL TODAY!	more days
day left	days 'til school
days	days to go …

4. Remove all the marker pins, and trim any excess thread.

Adding Hook-and-Loop Tape

Cut 6 squares from the hook side of hook-and-loop tape, and stitch each piece, faceup, around all 4 edges onto the calendar base. Each piece of the hook tape should be centered in the space to the left of the wording and to the right of the red margin line.

Finishing

1. Fold the length of thin ribbon in half to make a loop, and stitch it in place toward the top of the backing piece of craft felt.

2. Place the calendar base faceup on top of the backing piece so the loose ends of the ribbon loop are sandwiched between the 2 layers, and pin them both together.

3. Stitch along all 4 edges to join the 2 calendar pieces. Trim away any excess craft felt so both pieces are the same size and shape.

4. Press each counting square onto the square of hook tape on the calendar, initially with the number side hidden. You will not need to add any loop tape to the squares, as the felt attaches to the hook tape by itself just enough to not fall off.

5. To count down to the first day of school, turn over the globe square on day 6 beforehand so the number 5 is revealed. As each day passes, turn a square over, hiding the motif and revealing the number, until

there are no more days to go, and the countdown has reached 0.

This calendar can be reused for all your children, and I hope they have a wonderful start to their education!

note

If you need help with free-motion stitching, I have made a video tutorial, which is available on YouTube.
Go to youtube.com/user/lucykatecrafts and click on the Machine Embroidery video.

Santa's Slippers

Finished size: 2¾″ × 5¾″

Go ahead and snap up one of those yummy holiday charm packs to make these adorable shoes. Simple to make but big on impact, these slippers can be hung from a decorative garland and are the perfect size to hold a small treat or holiday message. Change the fabric and the number of shoes to suit any occasion, such as a sweet baby shower gift (with a onesie rolled into each shoe), a vacation/honeymoon (with travel-sized toiletries), or a quilting retreat (with a rolled fat quarter).

ARTIST: Carla Alexandra

Carla Alexandra was born in Portugal and has traveled the world through her work as a development worker. After adopting her child, she developed the need to create unique pieces for her daughter to play with and started using the different fabrics bought during her trips to Asia and Africa. The Great Craft Disaster brand was born.

EMAIL: carla@vendinha.net

WEBSITE: greatcraftdisaster.com

MATERIALS

6˝ × 5˝ scraps of fabric prints to make 25 shoes (Large-scale prints and prints with figures work well.)

¼ yard heavy-duty felt

⅜˝-wide numbered ribbon with the numbers 1–25

25 clothespins

Approximately 3 yards ½˝ decorative cord

tip

If you can't find ribbon preprinted with numbers, make your own by stamping or hand writing the numbers.

CUTTING

Using the patterns (page 100), trace and cut out 25 shoe soles from the felt and 25 shoe tops from the fabric prints. If you want to create pairs of shoes, then reverse the patterns for 12 of the shoes. (The last shoe will have no matching pair.)

CONSTRUCTION

1. Cut off a numbered piece of ribbon, and fold it in half.

2. Turn under the top edge of the shoe top a scant ³⁄₁₆˝. Press. Pin the numbered ribbon in place along the top edge of the shoe top. Stitch across the top, catching the ribbon along the way. Turn under the side edges a scant ³⁄₁₆˝, and press. Alternatively, serge the rounded side edges to finish them.

3. Place the shoe top on the sole, right sides up, aligning the outside edges. Straight stitch around the outside of the shoe top, through the sole and close to the edges, all around the curved edges. Leave the top numbered edge loose.

Finishing

1. Hang the decorative cord.

2. Hang the shoes in place with clothespins, and fill with treats.

A Bear for Baby

Finished size: 14″ tall (sitting), 25″ belly circumference

This bear is sure to be the hit of the baby shower with its apron full of goodies. Wrap and attach a variety of purchased baby essentials so that the mom-to-be can count down the days to baby's arrival. Instructions are provided to customize the apron to fit any stuffed critter. Plastic-coated spoons, gift cards, rattles, cloths, nail clippers, clothes, and hats are all great gifts to include, as well as gifts geared toward the mom-to-be, such as lotions and massage gift certificates.

Liz keeps herself busy as an editor, author, and designer. She loves to add texture to her sewing and quilting projects with dimensional elements: beads, buttons, hardware, findings, you name it—anything to add fun and interest.

EMAIL: liza@ctpub.com

ARTIST: Liz Aneloski

MATERIALS

Note: Adjust the fabric amount based on the size of the bear.

Stuffed bear

¾ yard print fabric for apron

Purchased visor

Graph paper

10 shank buttons (yellow or your choice of color)

11 buttons (shank or 2- or 4-hole, in red or your choice of color)

2 yards ⅛″-wide ribbon

8 round tags

Paper punch *(optional)*

Adhesive numbers 1–8

8 baby items

CUTTING

Note: Make an apron and pocket pattern for the bear before cutting the fabric (see Apron and Pocket Pattern, page 14).

Print fabric

Referring to the cutting layout diagram (below), fold the fabric in half crosswise, perpendicular to the selvages.

- Cut 2 strips 1½″ × fabric width for the shoulder and side straps; cut each strip in half to make 4 strap pieces 1½″ × approximately 20″.

- Cut out 2 apron pieces and 1 pocket piece, with the top edge of each piece on the fold of the fabric.

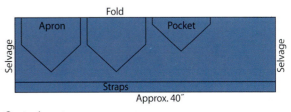

Cutting layout

APRON AND POCKET PATTERN

1. Measure your bear from armpit to armpit, and draw a horizontal line (Line 1) this length on the graph paper.

2. With the bear sitting, measure from the bear's chin to the tabletop, and draw a vertical line (Line 2) this length from the center of Line 1.

3. Measure from the bear's chin to its belly button area, even with its hips, and draw a vertical line (Line 3) from each end of Line 1.

4. Draw diagonal lines (Line 4) from both Line 3's, at about 45° angles, stopping where the drawn lines meet.

5. Draw a horizontal line (Line 5) 1˝ up from where Lines 3 and 4 come together to mark the top of the apron pocket.

6. Cut out the paper pattern (seam allowances are included).

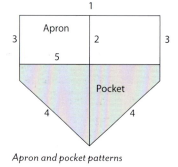

Apron and pocket patterns

CONSTRUCTION

Note: Use ¼˝ seam allowances unless otherwise noted.

1. Fold one of the apron pieces in half, right sides together. Stitch along the raw edges, leaving a 3˝ opening for turning. If desired, curve the bottom as I did.

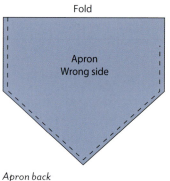

Apron back

2. Turn the apron right side out, press, and hand stitch the opening closed.

3. Open the other apron piece, and place it right side up on the work surface.

4. Add decorative stitching along the folded edge of the pocket, if desired.

5. Position the pocket piece (folded as it was cut, with wrong sides together), on top of the apron piece, aligning the bottom corners.

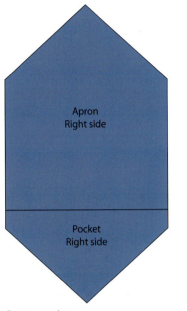

Position pocket.

6. Refold the apron with right sides together, aligning the bottom corners. The pocket is sandwiched between the layers.

7. Stitch along the raw edges, leaving a 3˝ opening for turning.

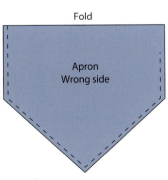

Apron front

8. Turn right side out, press, and hand stitch the opening closed.

9. Fold a strip piece in half crosswise (1½˝ × approximately 10˝), right sides together, and stitch both long raw edges, leaving the short end open for turning. Turn the strap right side out, and press. Repeat this step to make 4 straps.

10. Position the adhesive numbers on the tags.

11. Attach tags 1–4 onto the apron pocket by placing a shank button through the hole of the tag and stitching it onto the pocket. (If your tags do not have precut holes, then make holes with a paper punch.)

12. Attach the folded ends of the shoulder and side straps to the outside of the apron front with buttons.

13. Place the apron on the bear, adjust the straps to fit (with the ends of the straps underneath the apron back), and attach the straps with buttons. Trim off the excess strap fabric.

14. Position the remaining tags at the ends of the arms and legs, and attach them by placing a shank button through the hole of the tag and stitching it onto the bear. (See Step 11.)

15. Cut pieces of ribbon long enough to tie around 4 baby items. Stitch the midpoint of each ribbon to the bear next to the numbered tags on the arms and legs.

16. Tie the attached ribbons around the baby items, and then tie in bows. Place the remaining baby items in the front pocket.

17. Stitch the remaining buttons onto the visor.

Candy Cane Lane

Finished size: 25¾˝ × 25¾˝ with binding

Candy stripes and bells help give this Christmas countdown calendar all its charm. They also provide a great excuse to shop for some fun novelty Christmas fabric. The clever construction adds a dimensional aspect to the calendar, and the button numbers save time and can be attached sequentially or scattered randomly. If you are making this for a child under the age of three, skip the bells, and use numbers cut from felt or stamped to avoid the risk of choking.

ARTIST: Liz Aneloski

Liz keeps herself busy as an editor, author, and designer. She loves to add texture to her sewing and quilting projects with dimensional elements: beads, buttons, hardware, findings, you name it—anything to add fun and interest.

EMAIL: liza@ctpub.com

MATERIALS

⅝ yard Christmas print for pockets*

¾ yard red print for pocket backgrounds and border

¾ yard small red-and-white stripe for Four-Patch blocks, side and corner setting triangles, and binding

⅛ yard green print for inset strip

⅞ yard for backing

30˝ × 30˝ batting

25 jingle bells (12mm)

Number buttons 1–25 (by Dill Buttons of America)

¼ yard for hanging sleeve

*If you are using a directional print, you'll need 1¼ yards of Christmas print fabric.

CUTTING

Christmas print

- Cut 5 strips 3½˝ × fabric width. From these strips, cut 50 squares 3½˝ × 3½˝ for the pockets. If you are using a directional print, then cut 7 strips 5˝ × fabric width, and subcut into 50 squares 3½˝ × 3½˝, but cut the 3½˝ × 3½˝ squares *on point* for the pockets.

Red print

- Cut 3 strips 3½˝ × fabric width. From these strips, cut 25 squares 3½˝ × 3½˝ for the pocket backgrounds.

- Cut 4 strips 2½˝ × fabric width for the border. (Trim to size later.)

Small red-and-white stripe
Note: Follow this cutting order to ensure success.

- Cut 3 strips on the lengthwise grain (parallel to the selvages) 2˝ × fabric length for the Four-Patch blocks. From the leftover fabric, cut:

- 2 strips on the crosswise grain (90° to the selvages) 2˝ × fabric width for the Four-Patch blocks

- 2 squares 3˝ × 3˝; cut each in half diagonally for the corner setting triangles
- 4 squares 5½˝ × 5½˝; cut each in half diagonally twice for the setting triangles
- 4 strips 2¼˝ × fabric width for the binding

Green print

- Cut 4 strips 1˝ × fabric width for the inset strip.

Hanging sleeve

- Cut 1 strip 8˝ × fabric width for the hanging sleeve. (Trim to size later.)

CONSTRUCTION

Note: Use ¼˝ seam allowances unless otherwise noted.

Pocket

1. Place the 3½˝ × 3½˝ squares of Christmas print right sides together.

Note: If you are using a printed fabric with a directional design, make sure the design is right side up on the top corner of one square and upside down on the other square. When the corner flops down, the design will be right side up.

Design right side up

Design upside down

2. On the square with the design right side up, make a mark on the 2 top edges ¾˝ from the side corners.

Mark.   Mark.

3. Using a ¼˝ seam allowance, begin stitching at one mark, backstitch to secure the threads, and continue stitching along one side. Pivot at the corner, continue stitching along the second side to the second mark, and backstitch.

4. Clip the seam allowances at the marks to within 2 threads of the stitching. Trim the stitched corner to reduce the bulk so you get a nice square corner.

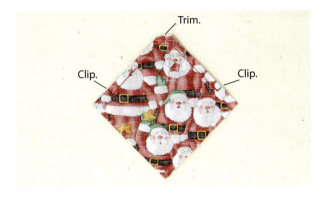

Trim.

Clip.　　Clip.

5. Turn the pocket right side out. Make sure the unstitched sections of the seam allowance are visible. Press.

6. Repeat Steps 1–5 to make 25 pockets.

Four-Patch Blocks

1. Cut 1 lengthwise strip of the stripe fabric in half. Stitch 1 of the half-strips to an end of each of the remaining 2 lengthwise strips.

2. Place 1 crosswise strip and 1 lengthwise strip of the stripe fabric right sides together.

3. Stitch along a long edge. Press in either direction. Repeat Steps 2–3 for the other 2 strips.

4. Trim 1 end of each strip set straight, and cut into a total of 32 units 2˝ wide.

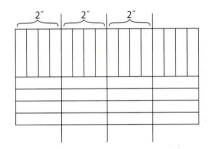

2˝　　2˝　　2˝

5. Stitch 2 of the units into a block so that the stripes in adjacent squares are oriented differently. Press. Make 16 blocks.

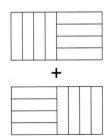

+

Quilt Top

1. Place a pocket (design oriented upright) on top of the right side of a background square. Line up the raw edges, and baste ⅛˝ from the raw edges. Make 25 blocks.

2. Arrange the blocks as shown in the quilt assembly diagram (at right).

3. Stitch the blocks into diagonal rows, adding the corner triangles. *Note: Be careful not to catch the finished edge of the pockets in the stitched seam.* Press.

4. Stitch the rows together. (See note in Step 3.) Press.

Borders

The quilt top should measure 21¾˝ × 21¾˝.

1. Fold each inset strip in half lengthwise, and press.

2. Trim 2 of the inset strips to 21¾˝ long.

3. Trim 2 of the border strips to 21¾˝ long.

4. Place a short folded inset strip along the top edge of the quilt top, aligning raw edges. Place a border strip on top of the inset strip, right sides together. Align the raw edges, and pin. Stitch, and press.

5. Repeat Step 4 for the bottom edge of the quilt top.

6. Trim the other 2 inset strips to 25¾˝ long.

7. Trim the other 2 border strips to 25¾˝ long.

8. As in Step 4, layer and pin the other inset strips with the other border strips on the sides of the quilt top. Stitch, and press.

Finishing

1. Layer, baste, and quilt.

2. Stitch the jingle bells to the tips of the pockets.

3. Stitch the number buttons onto the pocket backgrounds.

4. Bind the quilt, and add a hanging sleeve.

5. Fill the pockets with special treasures, and count down the days 'til Christmas.

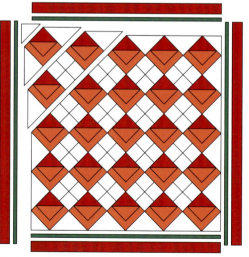

Quilt assembly diagram

Flip for Father's Day

Finished page size: 8˝ × 8˝
Finished display size: 8˝ × 13˝

Just about all of the components on this countdown are upcycled: the stand, the pockets from dress shirts, the buttons, and even one of the numbers! Use classic blue to count the days until Father's Day or crisp tones of white and cream to count the days until a wedding. Having just enough room for five individual sheets, this is perfectly suited for an occasion when you don't have many days to count down. Sew the sheets in rows, and you have a message center!

ARTIST: Sue Astroth

Sue Astroth is a native Californian who lives with her family in the Bay Area. She carves out a little time each day to work on her many crafting projects, even if it means getting up at 4 A.M. Knitting, sewing, paper crafting, cross-stitch, felting, and quilting are just some of the ways she expresses her creative talent. Some of her creations have been featured on the C&T blog as "Junk to Jewel."

EMAIL: suea@ctpub.com

MATERIALS

Photo stand (Mine was a vintage piece, but you can use a photo stand from 7 Gypsies—it comes with binding rings.)

5 sheets grunge paper (You may have to adjust the grunge paper size to fit your photo stand.)

White distress crackle paint

Numbers 1–5 (I cut some from grunge paper scraps; "5" is a vintage house number.)

5 tags/candy/treasures to add to each pocket

Assorted kids' collared shirts with pockets or 5 coordinating fabric scraps to make your own pockets

Assorted jeans or denim scraps in various sizes at least 8″ × 8″

Assorted embellishments and ribbons to go with your own style or theme

Japanese screw punch with ⅜″-hole bit (approximately)

2 binding rings, 3″ diameter (only if repurposing a found stand)

1 yard fusible web (*optional*)

Fabric glue as needed for numbers and embellishments

Scrap heavyweight paper or cardstock

CONSTRUCTION

1. Cut 5 sheets of grunge paper to size for your stand (mine were 8″ × 8″).

2. Using the white crackle paint, paint ½″ all the way around each grunge paper square, front and back, and let them dry.

3. Cut 5 denim squares ½″ smaller than the grunge paper base.

4. Cut out the pockets with a ½″ seam allowance on all sides. Turn under ¼″ on all 4 sides, and press.

5. Place each pocket on a square of denim, and stitch it in place.

6. Stitch or glue on the numbers, and add embellishments as desired.

7. Stitch each embellished denim square to a grunge paper square. If the fabric moves too much while stitching, iron a 5½″ × 5½″ square of fusible web onto the center back of the denim, fuse the fabric to the grunge paper, and then stitch around the edges.

8. Using a scrap of heavyweight paper or cardstock (for example, from the back of a notepad), make a template for where you want to punch the holes on the calendar pages. Test out the hole position on scraps before you punch the actual numbered pages.

9. Using the template and screw punch, drill holes in the countdown pages. Place the pages on rings, and set them onto the photo stand.

10. Add treasures to the pockets.

tip

Add additional denim layers under the pockets to add your own decorative flair.

Use colorful ribbons or scraps of fabric and purchased organza cinch-top bags to transform this common hardware store item into a festive treat holder. Adjust the colors for a favorite sports team to count the days to the big game, or use school colors for a graduation day count-down. This project is so simple, that the possibilities are endless!

All Tied Up

Finished size: approximately 4˝ × 36˝

Sue Astroth is a native Californian who lives with her family in the Bay Area. She carves out a little time each day to work on her many crafting projects, even if it means getting up at 4 A.M. Knitting, sewing, paper crafting, cross-stitch, felting, and quilting are just some of the ways she expresses her creative talent. Some of her creations have been featured on the C&T blog as "Junk to Jewel."

EMAIL: suea@ctpub.com

ARTIST: Sue Astroth

MATERIALS

17 yards or more of assorted ribbons in varying colors and widths (I used up a lot of ribbon scraps that were just too big to throw away. The more you tie on, the better!)

1 chain-link fence tie, about 36˝ long (heavy-gauge wire, bent in half and twisted together)

1 package of 10 organza pouches 3˝ × 4˝ in coordinating colors

Black spray paint *(optional)*

10 metal-rimmed tags

1 sheet scrapbook paper

Circle punch the size of the paper part of a metal-rimmed tag

Numbers 1–10 (I made mine from cardstock and my die-cut machine. You could easily use stickers or precut chipboard numbers.)

Enough candy or other treasures to fill organza bags

Fence tie

CONSTRUCTION

1. Spray the fence tie with your choice of color, and let it dry.

2. Cut ribbons into 6˝ lengths.

3. Using a single knot, attach the ribbon to the fence tie. Make sure to mix up the colors for a pleasing arrangement.

tips

- Tie the fence tie to a drawer handle or other stationary object so you are not trying to tie ribbons onto a moving object.

- When using ¼˝-wide ribbon, tie 2 strands of the same ribbon at the same time for added fullness.

4. Fill the organza bags with candy or other treats, and tie them onto the fence tie at even intervals.

5. Punch 10 circles from scrapbook paper, and glue them to the tags.

6. Glue the numbers to the tags, and tie them to the organza bags.

7. Trim the ribbon ends as necessary.

I made my countdown calendar large enough to run for 10 days. You could make the countdown calendar run for a longer period by using a longer length of fence tie or a piece of chain. Figure on about 17 yards of ribbon for each yard of fence tie or chain.

Coordinate the ribbon colors to match the event: a baby, a wedding, a birthday, or school beginning or ending. Or you could use larger organza bags (make your own) and use this as a prize stick.

Eight Days of Hanukkah

Finished sizes: 2″ wide × 2″ deep × varying heights (up to 10½″ tall)

Celebrate Hanukkah with a whimsical new twist on an old tradition. Make friendly houses or glitzy candles with translucent Lutradur. Either design can hold tiny gifts or Hanukkah *gelt* (foil-wrapped chocolate coins). Open one gift each day, and, if you wish, use a battery-operated tea light inside each candle.

ARTIST: Cynthia Bix

Cynthia is the author of many books for adults and children on subjects ranging from home decorating to natural science. Her personal essays have appeared in a variety of newspapers and magazines.

EMAIL: cynthiab@ctpub.com

Lynn is a fiber artist, author, and teacher. She has a short attention span, so she loves to try new products and techniques. Her current focus is dyeing and painting on fabric. She is the author of *Fast, Fun & Easy Fabric Dyeing* and *Fast, Fun & Easy Creative Fabric Clocks*.

ARTIST: Lynn Koolish

EMAIL: lynn@lynnkoolish.com
WEBSITES:
lynnkoolish.com
flickr.com/photos/lynnquilter

MATERIALS AND CUTTING

7 sheets 8½˝ × 11˝ of 70g or 100g Lutradur (*Note: Paint the Lutradur before cutting; see Painting, page 30.*)

- Cut 4 Lutradur sheets in half to make 8 base pieces 8½˝ × 5½˝.

- From 1 Lutradur sheet, cut 1 base piece 8½˝ × 8˝.

- From the remaining 2 Lutradur sheets:
  Cut 9 pairs of flame pieces (using the pattern, page 101) for the candles.

  or

  Cut 9 roof pieces (using the pattern, page 101) for the houses.

Acrylic paints (We used Liquitex Soft Body acrylic paints.)

Old tray or other work surface

Rubber work gloves

Plastic palette

Small fabric or painted Lutradur scraps for doors and windows

Embroidery floss in several colors *or* glue

Glitter glue

Press-on numbers approximately 1˝ high

Heat tool such as the Creative Textile Tool from Walnut Hollow (*optional*)

Battery-operated tea lights (*optional*)

CONSTRUCTION

Painting

Note: Paint the Lutradur before cutting out the pieces. For the houses, we used a blend of yellow and burnt sienna—reminiscent of the buildings in Jerusalem—and a reddish-brown for the roofs. For the candles, we painted 5 of the bases blue and left 4 unpainted, and we painted the flames yellow and orange with a touch of glitter glue.

Paint 5 of the Lutradur sheets for the house or candle bases, and paint the remaining 2 sheets for the house roofs or candle flames.

using acrylic paints

Mix acrylic paints to create the desired colors on the plastic palette. Place the Lutradur pieces on a protected surface, and spray the pieces with water to thoroughly dampen them. Use your fingers to apply paint evenly all over the surfaces, all the way out to the edges. Allow the Lutradur to dry.

Bases

Fold each base piece as shown. Use a ruler edge to make sharp creases.

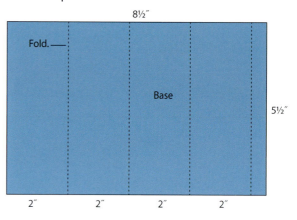

For Houses

1. Using the patterns (page 101) or cutting freehand, cut windows and doors from fabric or painted Lutradur scraps. Stitch them to the houses using 1 to 3 strands of embroidery floss in small running stitches. Add any embellishing stitches you wish. If you prefer, you can glue them instead.

2. Fold each roof piece along the dotted lines. Use embroidery floss in a running stitch to stitch together the seam, or use glue.

For Candles

1. Create a lace effect around the top edge of each base with a heat tool. Do this in a well-ventilated area, or work outside.

2. Cut slits in the flame pieces as marked on the pattern, and slot together a pair of pieces. Half of the flame pieces have slits cut from the top, and the other half have slits cut from the bottom so they fit together.

Finishing

1. Stitch together the vertical base seam using embroidery floss in a running stitch, or, if you prefer, glue the pieces together instead.

2. Press or glue the numbers firmly into position.

3. Place the house roofs or candle flames on top, and you're finished.

> ## tip
> Cut a square of foam core as an inside flat base for the houses and candles to keep them standing straight.

Holiday Activity Advent Calendar

Finished size: 13½" × 11"

If it is true that big surprises can come in small packages, this mini Christmas countdown calendar holds great promise. Designed to hold small bits of paper that list a fun holiday event or family tradition, this calendar adds festive spontaneity to the season. Messages listing "Go Caroling," "Bake Cookies," and "Watch *A Christmas Story*" are all possibilities. Add decorative trim, embroidered dates, and imaginative activities to make each day a surprise!

Sonia is a stay-at-home mom living in southern France. She started getting crafty about five years ago, initially with cross-stitch. She moved on to freehand embroidery and now enjoys using and mixing embroidery, linen, cotton prints, crocheted laces, and trims to make her creations.

EMAIL:
cozymemories@orange.fr

WEBSITES:
cozymemories.etsy.com
cozyhomemaking.blogspot.com
flickr.com/photos/cozymemories
twitter.com/cozymemories

ARTIST: Sonia Cantie

MATERIALS AND CUTTING

**½ yard cream linen for front and back;
cut 2 rectangles 14˝ × 11½˝**

**¼ yard natural linen for pockets;
cut 28 rectangles 1¾˝ × 2˝**

Assorted scraps of trims, ribbons, and rickrack

4 decorative buttons

Red embroidery floss

2 D-rings ¾˝ long

CONSTRUCTION

Note: Use ¼˝ seam allowances.

1. Embroider numbers on 24 of the pockets using 1 strand of red embroidery floss. Number them from 1 to 24.

2. Fold under the top of each embroidered pocket ¼˝, and press. Stitch a piece of trim to the top front edge.

3. Fold and stitch under the top edge (without any embellishment) of the 4 remaining pockets.

4. Stitch the buttons onto the 4 plain pockets.

5. On each pocket, cut out a small triangle from the 2 bottom corners, to avoid bulk when you turn under the edges. Fold under the 3 unstitched sides ¼˝, and press.

6. Arrange the 28 pockets on the front of a cream rectangle, pin the pockets in place, and sew them to the background, leaving the top of the pocket unstitched.

7. Place the 2 cream rectangles right sides together. Pin, and then stitch around the edges using a ¼˝ seam allowance, leaving 5˝ of the seam open for turning.

8. Turn the calendar right side out, press the seams, and stitch the opening closed. Topstitch around all 4 sides.

9. Stitch D-rings in the top corners of the back for hanging.

Crisp linen and textured fabrics make this calendar sophisticated, cozy, and fun. The simple instructions make this a breeze to sew, perfect for gift-giving. Use preprinted number ribbon to designate the days, or stamp or stitch numbers directly onto purchased ribbon to make this even more of a quick project. The small pockets are just the right size for little fingers to find little goodies inside.

Sophisticated Christmas

Finished size: 14˝ × 16˝

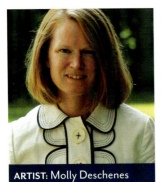

After having lived in far-flung places such as Budapest and Berlin, Molly Deschenes settled down in small-town New England with the love of her life and her sewing machine. At www.applecyder.com, she chronicles her sewing adventures and provides a window into the handmade life she shares with her husband and two small children.

ARTIST: Molly Deschenes

EMAIL: acyder@gmail.com
WEBSITE: applecyder.com

MATERIALS AND CUTTING

Notes: Use ¼˝ seam allowances unless otherwise noted. Width of linen assumed to be greater than 32˝.

¾ yard linen

- Cut 2 pieces 15˝ × 17˝ for background/backing.
- Cut 1 piece 12˝ × 4˝ for the hanging sleeve.

Low-loft batting

- Cut 1 piece 15˝ × 17˝.

½˝-wide ribbon

- Cut 2 pieces 17˝ long.

Assorted cotton prints

- Cut 25 squares 2½˝ × 2½˝ for the pocket fronts.

¼ yard neutral-color cotton

- Cut 25 squares 2½˝ × 2½˝ for the pocket lining.

Ribbon scraps at least 5˝ long

1 sheet neutral-color inkjet printer fabric

1 wooden dowel ⅜˝ diameter, 13½˝ long

CONSTRUCTION

Number Tabs

1. Pick your favorite font for numbers about ⁵⁄₁₆˝ high. Leave space on all sides of the numbers for room to cut the tabs (see Step 2, below). Following the instructions on the inkjet printer fabric package, print the numbers. If you like, use a contrasting color to mark Christmas and St. Nicholas Day (December 6).

2. Cut out the number tabs, leaving ½˝ blank space below each printed number. The number tabs that I cut out for this project were 1⅞˝ × ¾˝. It is important that the number be placed on the lower half of the tab.

3. Fold and press each tab so that the fold is above each number and the short raw edges are aligned.

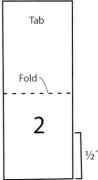

Pockets

1. Embellish the right side of the pocket front squares as desired. I topstitched ribbon to make some of the pockets look like gifts.

2. Arrange the pocket front squares in rows.

3. For each pocket, make a sandwich:

Place a lining fabric square right side up.

Place the appropriate folded number tab *number side up,* so that the short raw edges of the number tab are aligned with the top raw edge of the lining square, and the tab is either centered or at least ¼˝ away from either side of the lining square.

Place the pocket front square right side down, making sure that all the edges are aligned with the lining square.

4. Pin the sandwich together at the number tab, making sure that you secure all the layers.

5. Starting at the bottom of the pocket (the side opposite the side where the tab is secured) stitch around the perimeter of the pocket, leaving a 1˝ opening centered at the bottom for turning. Backstitch at the beginning and end of each seam.

6. Clip the excess fabric at the corners.

7. Turn the pocket right side out, and press, making sure that the extra fabric at the opening is pressed inside the pocket.

Assembling the Calendar

1. Arrange the pockets on the right side of the linen background. Leave a 1˝ border on the bottom and both sides, and a 2˝ border on the top.

2. Pin the pockets in place, and topstitch them down, leaving their top edges unstitched. Backstitch at the beginning and end of each seam. You will be closing the opening that was left for turning at the bottom of each pocket as you do this.

3. Make a quilt sandwich: Place the back of the calendar right side up, place the front of the calendar right side down, and then place the piece of batting on top. Pin the layers together all around.

4. Stitch around the perimeter of the calendar *using a ½˝ seam allowance,* and leaving an opening centered at the bottom for turning. Backstitch at the beginning and end of each seam.

5. Clip the excess fabric at the corners, and trim the excess batting that is in the seam allowance.

6. Turn the calendar right side out, and press, making sure that the extra fabric at the opening is pressed inside the calendar. Slipstitch the opening closed by hand.

7. Topstitch around the perimeter of the calendar.

Finishing

1. Fold the piece of linen for the sleeve in half lengthwise, with right sides together, and pin.

2. Stitch around the sides and bottom of the rectangle, leaving a 1˝ opening centered at the bottom for turning. Backstitch at the beginning and end of each seam.

3. Clip the excess fabric at the corner. Turn the sleeve right side out, and press, making sure that the fabric at the opening is enclosed.

4. Center the sleeve just below the top of the back of the calendar, and pin it in place.

5. Hand stitch the sleeve onto the back of the calendar, making sure that your stitches do not show through to the front of the calendar. Leave openings at the short ends of the sleeve so that you can slip a dowel through it.

6. Make a loop at one end of each piece of ribbon that you have set aside for hanging the calendar. Size the loops to fit the dowel. Stitch the loops closed.

7. Thread a dowel through the hanging sleeve. The dowel should be longer than the length of the hanging sleeve but shorter than the width of the calendar, so that it does not stick out past the side edges of the calendar and remains hidden from the front view. Trim the dowel if necessary.

8. Thread the ends of the dowel through the loops at the ends of the ribbon, and tie the other ends of the 2 pieces of ribbon in a bow.

9. Hang your calendar, and enjoy!

The Reason for the Season

Finished size: 23″ × 28″

Use the same construction technique as the Holiday Activity Advent Calendar (page 32) to sew this variation, but embellish with lace, buttons, rickrack, and embroidery for a vintage look, and add a meaningful message to the top of a gathered fabric banner.

ARTIST: Elizabeth Letourneau

Elizabeth Letourneau is a happily married mother of two who loves vintage silver, granny squares, and anything of the dusty, thrifted variety. She'd love to have you by for tea at her coastal Massachusetts home—just call first so she can straighten up a bit.

EMAIL: elizsleto@verizon.net
WEBSITE: flickr.com/photos/my-crafty-mess/

Birthday Cake Countdown

Finished size: 13″ × 23½″

No one will be able to wait until his or her birthday to display this festive and thoughtful calendar. One felt candle is in each of the pockets and can be placed onto the cake each day. A "Happy Birthday" banner snaps to the top for an added bit of whimsy. Combine felt, fabric, rickrack, and stamping to create this fourteen-day countdown. Include a small gift, note, or fabric crown in the "today" pocket.

ARTIST: Erin Ermish

Erin lives in beautiful North Carolina with her wonderful husband, Gary, and her rescued Siberian huskies, Chance and Bleu. When she began creating things for her family and friends as gifts, she found that other people actually liked her designs. That was when she decided to make her creations available to others, and CrazyHuskyCrafts was born. Her two huskies are her constant companions when her husband is away on business, so honoring them seemed like the perfect thing to do when she needed a name for her business.

EMAIL: erinchaney@mindspring.com

WEBSITE: etsy.com/shop/CrazyHuskyCrafts

MATERIALS AND CUTTING

1 fat quarter brown fabric for calendar background

- Cut 1 piece 11˝ × 5½˝ (Row 1).
- Cut 2 pieces 3¾˝ × 3½˝ (Row 2).
- Cut 2 pieces 2¾˝ × 3½˝ (Row 3).
- Cut 2 pieces 1¾˝ × 3½˝ (Row 4).
- Cut 2 pieces 11˝ × 2½˝ (Rows 6 and 7).
- Cut 2 pieces 3½˝ × 2½˝ (Row 8).
- Cut 1 piece 5˝ × 2½˝ (Row 8).

1 fat quarter blue dot fabric for cake

- Cut 1 piece 4½˝ × 3½˝ (Row 2).
- Cut 1 piece 6½˝ × 3½˝ (Row 3).
- Cut 1 piece 8½˝ × 3½˝ (Row 4).

1 fat quarter solid green fabric for cake stand

- Cut 1 piece 11˝ × 1½˝ (Row 5).
- Cut 1 piece 2˝ × 4˝ (pockets, Rows 6 and 7).
- Cut 1 piece 5˝ × 2˝ (bottom pocket, Row 8).

¼ yard blue-and-green plaid fabric for border

- Cut 2 pieces 11˝ × 1½˝.
- Cut 2 pieces 1½˝ × 23½˝.

½ yard lining and backing fabric

- Cut 2 pieces 11˝ × 2˝ (pocket lining, Rows 6 and 7).
- Cut 1 piece 5˝ × 2˝ (pocket lining, Row 8).
- Cut 1 piece 14˝ × 25˝ for the backing.

Scraps of 3 blue fabrics each measuring at least 2˝ × 8˝ for pockets (Rows 6 and 7)

- Cut 2 pieces 2˝ × 4˝ from each of the scraps.

Scraps of felt for candles and banner

14˝ × 25˝ batting

14 hook-and-loop dots, ⅝˝ diameter

20˝ medium-orange rickrack

24˝ double-fold bias binding, ¼˝ wide

4˝ cotton tape (ribbon), ½˝ wide

4 sew-on snaps

Fabric glue

Numbers stamp

CONSTRUCTION

Note: Use ¼˝ seam allowances.

Cake

1. Cut the rickrack into 3 pieces measuring 4½˝, 6½˝, and 8½˝ long. Baste a piece of rickrack close to the top edge of each piece of blue dot fabric on the front side.

2. Row 2: Stitch a 3¾˝ × 3½˝ piece of brown fabric to each of the short sides of the 4½˝ × 3½˝ piece of blue dot fabric. Press toward the brown fabric.

3. Row 3: Stitch a 2¾˝ × 3½˝ piece of brown fabric to each of the short sides of the 6½˝ × 3½˝ piece of blue dot fabric. Press toward the brown fabric.

4. Row 4: Stitch a 1¾˝ × 3½˝ piece of brown fabric to each of the short sides of the 8½˝ × 3½˝ piece of blue dot fabric. Press toward the brown fabric.

Pockets (Rows 6 to 8)

1. Rows 6 and 7: *With the light green fabric as the middle piece,* stitch each of the 6 blue pieces and 1 green piece together along the 4˝ sides to create 1 piece measuring 11˝ × 4˝.

2. Cut the unit made in Step 1 into 2 strips measuring 11˝ × 2˝. These are used to form the 2 rows of pockets.

3. Stamp numbers for the countdown on each pocket, referring to the photo on page 44 for placement.

tip

To make the placement of the numbers even, I measured ¼˝ from the left side and ½˝ from the bottom of each pocket. For the left pockets 7 and 14, I measured ½˝ from the left and bottom of the pocket.

4. With right sides together, stitch an 11˝ × 2˝ pocket lining strip to a pocket strip from Step 2 along the top long edge. Press the seam allowances open, and fold the front of the pocket down along the seam-line so the pocket lining and pocket front have their wrong sides together. Press. Topstitch ⅛˝ from the folded edge.

5. Place the unit from Step 4 on top of the pocket background (the brown fabric piece measuring 11˝ × 2½˝), with right sides facing up and aligning the bottom raw edges; baste in place. To create the pockets, stitch along the vertical seamlines for each of the pockets.

6. Repeat Steps 4 and 5 for the second row of pockets.

7. For Row 8: For the bottom pocket, stamp the letters "T-o-d-a-y" on the right side of the green piece of fabric measuring 5˝ × 2˝. With right sides together, stitch this piece and the 5˝ × 2˝ piece of lining fabric together along the top long edge, and press the seam open. Fold the pocket front down so the pocket lining and pocket front fabrics have their wrong sides together. Press. Topstitch ⅛˝ from the folded edge.

8. Baste the "Today" pocket to the 5˝ × 2½˝ piece of brown fabric, aligning the bottom raw edges. Press. Stitch a 3½˝ × 2½˝ piece of brown fabric to each side of the pocket you just created. Press toward the brown fabric.

Assembly

1. Stitch together Rows 1–8, pressing as you sew.

2. Stitch the short top and bottom borders to the quilt. Press.

3. Stitch the left and right borders to the quilt. Press.

4. Center and baste the ends of the 4˝-long piece of cotton tape to the top of the calendar as a hanger. At this stage, the short ends point up, away from the center of the quilt.

5. Layer the batting, the calendar (right side up), and the backing fabric (wrong side up). Be sure the hanger is between the calendar front and the backing fabric. Stitch the layers together, leaving a 6˝ gap at the bottom for turning. Trim the batting and backing even with the quilt top.

6. Turn the calendar right side out, and press. Turn in the seam allowance at the opening ¼˝, and press. Topstitch around the entire calendar, ⅛˝ from the edge, to finish.

Candles

1. Trace 14 candles (see Patterns, page 107) onto the back side of the felt. Cut along the traced line. Glue one side of a hook-and-loop dot to the back of each candle.

2. Glue the matching pieces of hook-and-loop dots to the cake (just above the rickrack) so that there are 3 candles on the top of the cake, 5 candles on the middle layer, and 6 candles on the bottom layer.

Banner

1. Trace a total of 13 triangles (see Patterns, page 107) onto the back side of the felt. Cut along the traced lines. Stamp each of the triangles to create the phrase "Happy Birthday."

2. Cut 2 pieces of double-fold bias binding measuring 12˝ long. Insert the "Happy" triangles into one piece of the cut binding, and topstitch along the open edge to hold the letters in place. Insert the "Birthday" triangles into the other cut piece of binding, and topstitch along the open edge to hold the letters in place.

tip

To keep the triangles from moving as you stitch, use a small dab of fabric glue to hold them in place.

Assembly diagram

3. Fold each end of the double-fold binding over ¼˝ toward the back of the banner, and stitch 1 snap at the end of each piece.

4. For the "Happy" banner, measure 1˝ in from the right edge, and stitch on a snap. For the "Birthday" banner, measure ¾˝ in from the right edge and 2¼˝ from the top, and stitch on the second snap. Repeat for both banners on the left side of the calendar.

To start your countdown, place a candle in each of the numbered pockets and the "Happy Birthday" banners in the "Today" pocket. Begin your count-down by placing a candle on the cake each day, and end your countdown by hanging the "Happy Birthday" banner at the top of the calendar on the big day.

Use upcycled uniforms or other old, but well-loved, items of clothing to add personalization to this improvisationally pieced project. Whether from a long posting overseas, or a short business trip, this calendar will help count down the days until a loved one returns home. No templates are provided here, but directions for how to piece the house are included.

Military Homecoming

Finished size: 22˝ × 10½˝ with binding

ARTIST: Jen Eskridge

Designer Jen Eskridge has been quilting for fifteen years and sewing for a bit longer. She is a military spouse—the wife of a fabulous guy currently on active duty in the Kansas Air National Guard. Jen graduated from Louisiana State University in 1998 with an apparel design degree, which she uses daily while working on quilting and sewing patterns for her company, ReannaLily Designs.

EMAIL: reannalilydesigns@hotmail.com
WEBSITE: reannalilydesigns.com

MATERIALS

Assorted large fabric scraps up to about 8½˝ × 10½˝ for house, sky, grass, and background rectangles

¼ yard or scraps of military uniform fabric, either from an old uniform or off the bolt

1 sheet 8½˝ × 11˝ of white felt

2 sheets 8½˝ × 11˝ of felt in contrasting color for numbers/letters

26˝ × 15˝ piece of batting

½ yard fabric for binding and backing

Buttons (*optional*)

Embroidery floss (*optional*)

CONSTRUCTION

Note: Use ¼˝ seam allowances unless otherwise noted. Draft freehand, print from your computer, or use a scrapbook die-cutting machine to produce the "n" and the felt letters and numbers in this project.

Home

1. Stitch together the ends of 2 scrap rectangles to create the door. Press, and trim the right and left sides of the piece to create straight lines. The sides do not need to be parallel to each other.

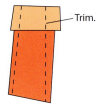
Trim.

2. Stitch a rectangle scrap to each side of the door. Ideally, these fabric scraps will either match or be the same color value as the piece of fabric above the door. These pieces form the main body of the house. Press, and trim the right and left sides again to give the house a pleasing shape.

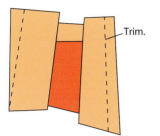

3. Stitch the sky fabric to the right and left sides of the house. The sky fabric should be as long as or longer than the existing house. Press, and trim the top and bottom of the house/sky unit. The top and bottom do not need to be parallel.

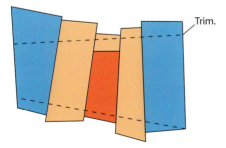

4. Build the roof of the house by cutting a triangle from military fabric with one side at least as wide as the top of the house. Stitch a large sky piece to the upper right side of the triangle. Trim the sky piece flush with the remaining triangle side.

5. Stitch the second sky piece to the left-hand side of the triangle. Trim the lower edge flush with the lower edge of the triangle. This complete roof/sky unit should be wider than the house/sky unit.

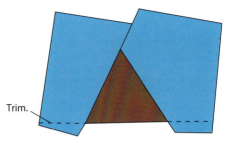

6. Center the triangle of the roof unit on the house, and stitch together the pieces. Press. Add a final grass piece to the lower edge of the house.

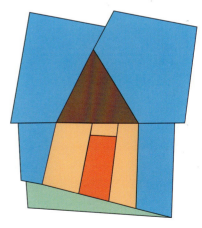

7. Trim the entire house block to a rectangular shape, with all sides intersecting at 90° angles. Make a note of the finished house block size. As a guide, the house block in the sample measures 8¼˝ × 10½˝ (cut size). Use the actual measurements of your house block to cut additional background rectangles for the "n" block and the "days" block (below and at right).

8. Draw, or have your child draw, a chunky heart shape onto military fabric. Cut out the heart and stitch it directly onto the house block.

"N" Block

1. Piece together 2 fabric scraps to create a background rectangle large enough to complement the house block. For reference, my "n" block background was pieced from 2 scraps cut to 3˝ × 10½˝ and 4˝ × 10½˝.

2. Draft, have your children draw, or use the computer to print a large lowercase letter "n." The "n" should be complementary in size to the house.

3. Trace the "n" onto military fabric, and then cut out and appliqué the "n" to the scrap block background.

Days

1. Cut the final fabric background block, and plan its dimensions for 2 functional rectangles on the right side of the background block, without overlapping the seam allowances. One rectangle is from white felt, for adhering the numbers, and the other is from military fabric and is large enough for the word "days." My background rectangle measures 8¼˝ × 10½˝ (cut size).

2. Cut the white felt rectangle to the determined size, and stitch around the perimeter to hold it in place on the background fabric.

3. From the contrasting color of felt, cut out, and stitch (or have your children glue) the letters "d-a-y-s" onto the military fabric rectangle. Appliqué the military fabric rectangle to the background block below the felt rectangle.

4. From the contrasting color of felt, cut out the numbers 0–9, cutting out more than one of each numeral, as needed, to count the remaining days.

Finishing

1. Stitch together the 3 large blocks, and press.

2. Measure the 3-block unit. From the backing fabric, cut a large rectangle 4˝ larger in each direction than the pieced top to use as the calendar back.

3. Layer the back, batting, and top for quilting. Pin baste the 3 layers, and quilt as desired.

4. Trim the backing and batting even with the calendar top.

5. Make a pocket to hold all the additional numbers by cutting a scrap into a rectangle 6˝ × 4˝. Fold the top long edge ¼˝ toward the wrong side twice. Press, and stitch the folded hem in place. Fold the right-hand edge of the pocket once ¼˝ toward the wrong side, and press. This edge will be hand stitched to the calendar back.

6. Working on the back, baste the pocket to the lower left corner of the project with the outside edges aligned. Hand stitch the right edge to the calendar backing. Do not stitch though to the front of the quilt when hand stitching.

7. Make binding, and stitch it around the calendar perimeter. The binding will conceal the left and bottom edges of the back pocket.

Consider stitching a label to the back of the calendar to mark every time your family has used this calendar. It will be an amazing piece of your family history.

You've Been Framed

Finished size: 18″ × 24″
(without framed edges)

Search out a thrift store frame or purchase a new one to hold this creative calendar. The black background provides a dramatic and modern background to the 25 fabric pockets, which can be adjusted in size to hold larger or smaller items. Personalize the frames with stencils or felt for a custom gift.

ARTIST: Linda Feldman

Before her first son was born, Linda worked as a school-based occupational therapist, assisting children who had difficulty functioning in the classroom. After becoming the mother and homeschooler of three boys, Linda found stitching to be therapeutic in maintaining her sanity. A designer of sewing patterns, she loves designing fun, functional items. It gives her great satisfaction to see others creating Craft Apple designs for themselves.

EMAIL:
lindiepindie@gmail.com

WEBSITES:
craftapple.com
craftapple.wordpress.com

MATERIALS

½ yard fabric 1 for pocket front

½ yard fabric 2 for pocket interior

1 yard fabric for background

1 yard fusible interfacing (or enough to cover 26˝ × 32˝)

1 yard paper-backed fusible web, 17˝ wide, such as HeatnBond Lite

Patterned cardstock for "JOY" lettering

Patterned cardstock for printing numbers 1–25

1½˝ circle punch

Standard frame with 18˝ × 24˝ opening, glass removed

Cardboard backing, about 20˝ × 26˝

Wide packing tape

Stapler and staples

3 pushpins

CONSTRUCTION

Circle and letter patterns are on page 103.

1. Create the fused fabric for the pockets by ironing the fusible web to the *wrong* side of fabric 1. After the fabric has cooled, remove the paper backing, and discard. Place fabric 1 against fabric 2, *wrong* sides together, and spread the pieces flat. Following the manufacturer's directions, iron to fuse the fabrics together.

2. Cut out 24 circles from the fused fabric using the 4˝ circle pattern. Cut out 1 circle from the fused fabric using the 5˝ circle pattern.

3. Create the fold in the pockets by measuring down 1½˝ from the top edge of the circle. Fold the top portion of the circle down at this spot so the right sides are together. Press the fold in place. Repeat for the remaining pocket pieces.

4. To finish the pockets, topstitch along the fold, ⅛˝ in from the edge, backstitching at the beginning and end. This flat edge is the top of the pocket. Repeat with all the remaining pocket pieces.

5. Prepare the background piece by cutting 1 piece of fabric 26˝ × 32˝. Fuse the interfacing to the *wrong* side of the background fabric. Fold the background piece in half lengthwise, and mark the midline by gently pressing with your fingers. Fold the background piece in half widthwise, and mark the other midline.

6. Arrange the pockets on the background piece, lining up the midpoint lines as a guide. Be sure to allow for a top margin of at least 5˝ and a bottom margin of at least 4˝. The side margins should be a minimum of 4˝. Pin the pockets in place using 2 pins per pocket to prevent rotation. Stitch them down by stitching around the curved part of the pocket, backstitching at the beginning and end.

7. From the *back* side of the frame, measure the opening of the frame. Cut the cardboard backing piece to this size.

8. Center the background piece with the pockets on the cardboard backing, wrap the fabric around to the back, and tape the fabric in place with the wide packing tape. There should be at least 2˝ clearance above the top row of pockets. Press the fabric-wrapped cardboard into the frame. If necessary, trim the fabric on the back of the frame to reduce bulk. Attach the outer frame backing to the back of the frame using the existing hardware.

9. Cut out the letters "J," "O," and "Y" from patterned cardstock. Position them at the top of the Advent calendar, and pin them in place with pushpins.

10. Create numbers for the pockets by printing numbers onto patterned cardstock and cutting them out using a 1½˝ circle punch.

11. Attach the numbers to the front of the pocket flaps using a stapler.

Fill with Advent surprises, and enjoy!

Any bride will love this pocketed wallhanging to commemorate all the different planning stages for her special day. The unique accordion-style design allows the entire calendar to be easily folded and stored as a keepsake, and allows for the addition of any number of pockets to suit. This design can be used for any countdown that has tasks and paperwork associated with it, like a move, a party, a vacation, a family reunion, or a large sewing project.

Wedding Day Pockets

Finished size: approximately 10˝ × 42˝

Lisa Fulmer works in marketing and spends much of her spare time creating fiber arts, mixed media, and paper-craft designs. She hosts a weekly webcast for artists, crafters, sewers, and quilters. Her work has been featured in two C&T books, *Cupcakes!* and *Color Your World with Princess Mirah Batiks.*

ARTIST: Lisa Fulmer

EMAIL: lisa@lisalizalou.com

WEBSITE: lisalizalou.com

MATERIALS AND CUTTING

Supplies are for one pocket panel.

1 rectangle 10˝ × 7˝ of heavyweight fast2fuse (by C&T Publishing)

1 rectangle 20˝ × 14˝ of black cotton fabric for background

1 rectangle 9¼˝ × 5¾˝ of 100g Lutradur, cut with pinking blade

Pale tan spritz ink (*optional*; not needed if white Lutradur looks good with your fabric choices)

1 rectangle 6¼˝ × 4˝ of brown netting, cut with pinking blade

1 rectangle 5¾˝ × 3½˝ of black/cream toile fabric, cut with pinking blade

1 rectangle 5¾˝ × 3½˝ of clear organza fabric

4 deep gold grommets (The last panel at the bottom only requires 2.)

2 pieces of coordinating grosgrain ribbon, 10˝ long

1 rectangle 2¾˝ × 1½˝ of cream muslin

1 sheet TAP (Transfer Artist Paper by C&T Publishing)

Decorative pearl-tipped pin

Rotary cutter with pinking blade

Heavy-duty hole punch (such as a Crop-A-Dile or Japanese screw punch)

Craft knife (such as an X-ACTO knife)

Bone folder

Gluestick

⅜˝ × 14˝ wood dowel

CONSTRUCTION

Directions are for one pocket panel.

Background

1. Place the fast2fuse in the center of the wrong side of the black fabric. Following the manufacturer's directions, fuse the fabric to the fast2fuse. Wrap and fuse the 2 long sides of the fabric to the back.

2. Miter the corners, wrap the short sides of the fabric to the back of the fast2fuse, and anchor stitch in the center. I used a 4½˝ vertical line of machine straight stitching to anchor the fabric in place for each short side. (The pocket covers the anchor stitches on the front.)

3. Punch 4 holes at the corners, centering them about ⅝˝ inside the long edges and about 1⅜˝ in from the vertical edges. Make the holes larger with the craft knife if needed. Insert and set the grommets. To plan ahead, if you are making several pockets to hang in a column, there is no need for ribbons or grommets at the bottom of the last panel.

Pocket

1. Spritz one side of the Lutradur with the ink color, and allow it to dry.

2. Enlarge the pocket pattern (page 102) 200%, and trace the outline onto the Lutradur. Cut the 2 slits. Put this aside.

3. Center and adhere the netting to the back of the toile rectangle with a gluestick.

4. Center and adhere the organza to the front of the toile rectangle with a gluestick.

5. Stitch the toile unit to the top center area of the Lutradur pocket, on the right side.

6. Use the dimensions given on the pocket pattern as guides to fold the Lutradur along the indicated lines. (Note that the ½˝-wide shaded strips on the pattern allow the pocket to protrude from the black background. They provide the depth so that you can fill the pockets.) To fold, first fold wrong sides together along both inner vertical fold lines. Crease with a bone folder. Next, fold right sides together along both outer vertical fold lines. Crease.

7. Fold wrong sides together twice horizontally at the bottom of the pocket at the first and second fold lines. Crease.

8. Referring to the illustration (below), place the pocket upside down on the background with right sides together. Center the bottom of the pocket about 1¼˝ up from the bottom of the background. Stitch across the bottom of the pocket.

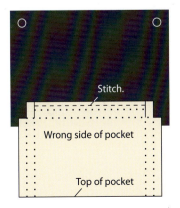

Stitch.

Wrong side of pocket

Top of pocket

9. Bring the top of the pocket up, tuck in the bottom corner flaps, square the bottom corners, and stitch the sides of the pocket to the background near the outside edges so that the stitching shows. (Zigzag stitching looks cute against the pinked edges of the Lutradur.)

10. Using your favorite computer font, print the word describing the pocket contents in reverse on TAP. (For reference, my letters are 24-point Zapfino font, and I used black type inside a cream box using Microsoft Word.)

11. Iron the TAP word to the muslin, and attach it to the pocket with the decorative pin.

12. Repeat Steps 1–11 to make as many panels as desired. Thread ribbon through each grommet to tie one panel to another. Ribbons at the top of the first panel slip over a dowel to hang on the wall.

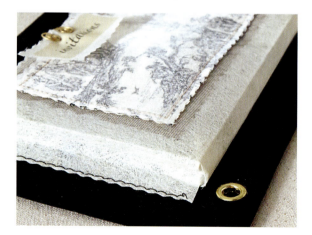

This project can be whipped up quickly and easily in an effort to organize chores in your family. The interactive process of pulling completed chore tabs out and flipping them for words of praise adds a dash of fun. As the kids sweat their way to the end of the week, their award waits to be revealed. Printing fresh new chores and awards maintains excitement. The cutout head on the hanger adds both humor and chart identification.

Chore Challenge

Finished size: 10˝ × 15˝

ARTIST: Tristan Gallager

Creating things of any kind is bliss for Tristan. Every medium yells potential, whether it's fiber, fabric, paint, paper, metal, wood, or found objects. For twelve years she has owned and run a custom gift business in San Francisco, while raising and instilling a passion for creativity in her children.

EMAIL: tristan427@gmail.com

MATERIALS AND CUTTING

1 rectangle 10˝ × 15˝ textured solid fabric for background

1 rectangle 12½˝ × 17½˝ coordinating fabric for backing

1 strip 1½˝ × 7˝ coordinating solid for letters and star (Or change it up by using a bright color for the star, or back the letters with a 1˝ square of contrasting fabric; *all optional.*)

1 rectangle 10˝ × 15˝ fast2fuse (by C&T Publishing)

5 rectangles 1¾˝ × 4˝ and 1 rectangle 2˝ × 4˝ of clear vinyl, such as Quilter's Vinyl (by C&T Publishing))

1 strip 1½˝ × 7˝ fusible web

Coordinating color thread

2 large grommets

Heavy-duty hole punch, ⅜˝ diameter

Ribbon or yarn for hanger

CONSTRUCTION

1. Center the background fabric right side up onto fast2fuse, and adhere according to the manufacturer's instructions.

2. Sew the top 1¾˝ × 4˝ vinyl sleeve into place. Align it 3˝ from the left side of the background and 1⅜˝ from the top. Leave the right side open for the chore cards to slip in and out. Sew the sleeve in place close to the edges on both long edges and on the left-hand vertical side. Place the next vinyl sleeve ¼˝ below the first, and sew it in place. Continue to add the remaining vinyl sleeves, placing the largest one on the bottom.

tips with vinyl

- Use a rug liner strip of rubber under the vinyl sleeve to prevent slippage.

- Use a walking or Teflon presser foot or place adhesive tape under the presser foot (cut a hole with an X-ACTO knife for the needle).

3. Back the letter/star fabric with fusible web. Cut into 6 squares 1˝ × 1˝. Using your favorite computer font or drawing freehand, draw and cut out 1 star and a letter for each day of the week in block style (M, T, W, T, F).

4. Mark (using a pin) 1˝ from the left side of the background, and center the letters and the star between the mark and the left edge of the vinyl sleeve. Fuse the letters in place on the background. *Optional:* Use coordinating-colored thread to sew a narrow zigzag stitch around the edges of the letters.

5. On the back side of the project, center the backing fabric on fast2fuse, and iron it according to the manufacturer's instructions. Flip the project faceup. Press a ¼˝ hem around all 4 edges of the background, and then fold over the left and right sides to the front, and press. Repeat for the top and bottom edges to create a border. Sew in place just inside the inner edges of the border.

6. Punch a hole near each top corner of the project, and insert 2 grommets. Attach hanging ribbons of the desired length to hang from a nail or other hanging device.

7. Make the chore tabs as follows. Using graphic software, create 5 rectangles 1˝ × 8½˝. One side of each tab shows the name of the chore, and the other side shows the praise message (be sure to flip to this side when the chore is done). After printing the chore names and praise messages on cardstock, cut out each rectangle, fold each in half, and glue the inside to create two-sided cards for sliding in and out of the sleeves.

Sample praise messages/symbols: "Good job!" "Good work!" "Way to go!" "You rock!"; check marks, graphic stars

Chores: Sweep, Dishes, Garbage, Set table, Bedroom

Yo-Yo Advent Tree

Finished size: 24˝ × 36˝

This calendar says Christmas through and through, and stands as a decoration all on its own. This project is big on handwork with the yo-yos, six different styles of ornaments, and buttons, but the result is big on fun. Not suitable for children under the age of three, but perfectly suitable for giving as a gift that will surely become a treasured family heirloom. Gather your scraps to make the yo-yos, and start early!

ARTIST:
Wendy "Sunshine" Harbaugh

Her real name is Wendy Harbaugh, but her nickname is "Sunshine." She is what's known as a fiber artist. She has a bachelors in fine arts from Brigham Young University and a minor in art history She also has two associate degrees in fine arts and liberal arts. Even with the art degrees, most things she does are self-taught. While taking care of her family, Wendy loves to design and make handmade items. Besides quilting, she also does crochet, knit, tat, bobbin lace, rug-making, bead-work, needle lace, ... the list goes on and on. In her spare time, she enjoys substitute teaching grades K–12. She believes that all people can make things with their hands—it just takes the desire and the time to learn the skill.

EMAILS:
sunshine_harbaugh@juno.com
sunshine.harbaugh@gmail.com

WEBSITES:
sunshinescreations.vintagethreads.com
etsy.com/shop/VintageThreads
facebook.com/pages/Sunshines-Creations/104230882941628
flickr.com/photos/sunshinescreations/
ravelry.com/people/sunshineharbaugh

MATERIALS

1⅛ yards white fabric for background and sleeve

⅓ yard each of 6 light red fabrics for border

6″ × 22″ pieces of 2 red fabrics for pot

¼ yard each of 6 light green fabrics for tree

⅝ yard dark green fabric for grass

6″ × 6″ scrap of brown fabric for square tree trunk

6″ × 6″ scrap of yellow fabric for star

Small Clover yo-yo flower maker for making yo-yo star (*optional*)

67 buttons

Note: See Ornaments (pages 63–66) for materials for and construction of the ornaments.

CUTTING

Note: See the yo-yo circle pattern (page 104), or trace a CD.

White
- Cut 1 piece 9″ × 21″ for the hanging sleeve.
- Cut 86 yo-yos for the background.

Light red
- Cut 60 yo-yos for the border.

Red
- Cut 7 yo-yos for the pot.

Light green
- Cut 42 yo-yos for the tree.

Dark green
- Cut 25 yo-yos for the grass.

Brown
- Cut 1 yo-yo for the trunk.

Yellow
- Cut 1 yo-yo for the star.

Yo-Yos

HOW TO MAKE A YO-YO

1. Trace the CD or the circle pattern (page 104) on the fabrics, and cut them out.

2. Knot the ends of a double strand of thread that matches the fabric. Fold over a ¼˝ seam allowance all around the yo-yo, and stitch a running stitch all around, close to the edge. Make the stitches relatively large so the yo-yo will close (see Step 3).

3. Pull the thread tight to gather the yo-yo, and tie a knot to secure.

4. Weave in the tail, and cut the thread.

HOW TO MAKE A YO-YO STAR

Use a Clover yo-yo flower maker to make the star, or use the following instructions.

1. Follow Steps 1–3 of How to Make a Yo-Yo (above).

2. Pass the thread to the back of the yo-yo, through the center. Bring the thread over the outside edge of the yo-yo to the front and then through the center to the back. This will form a shape similar to a heart the first time only.

3. Repeat Step 2 until you have a star shape.

4. Tie a knot on the back of the star, and cut the thread.

CONSTRUCTION

Wallhanging

1. Make the yo-yos.

2. Arrange the yo-yos into 21 rows, placing the yo-yos face down (smooth side up). Refer to the photo (page 60) as needed for placement.

3. Stitch the yo-yos together. Save the star until last, and stitch it on top of the tree.

4. Stitch a button in the middle of every green yo-yo on the quilt to hang the ornaments.

Hanging Sleeve

1. Fold the white 21˝ × 9˝ strip in half, right sides together, making a strip that is 21˝ × 4½˝.

2. Stitch with a ½˝ seam allowance down the length of the strip.

3. Fold over ½˝ twice at both short ends of the stitched tube so that the raw edges are enclosed, and stitch those hems.

4. Rotate the sleeve so the long seam is hidden, and stitch the sleeve to the back of the wallhanging along both long edges.

ORNAMENTS

Adorn your tree with six different ornaments (pages 64–66).

Holly and Berries

MATERIALS

Green felt in multiple shades

Red and green perle cotton thread

Red glass beads

CONSTRUCTION

1. Use the holly pattern (page 104) to cut 2 or 3 leaves for each ornament you want to make.

2. Embroider the leaves in green perle cotton using a stem stitch.

3. Arrange the leaves, and stitch the beads in place with red perle cotton. Use the same thread to make a hanging loop, knotting it on the back side of the ornament.

Jingle Bell Candy Canes

MATERIALS

White and red pipe cleaners

Red or green perle cotton thread

Jingle bells

Wire cutters

CONSTRUCTION

1. Twist 2 pipe cleaners together, 1 white and 1 red, and cut them into 3˝ segments.

2. Wrap 1 end of the twisted pipe cleaners over a pencil or pen to create the curve in the hook of the cane.

3. Thread the perle cotton through the jingle bell, and tie a knot.

4. Place the candy cane on the threads, and pass the knotted end through the thread circle near the bell. Pull tight to make a hanging loop.

Mint Candies

MATERIALS

White felt scraps

Red or green perle cotton thread

Decorative brads

Beads, sequins, glitter, or confetti *(optional)*

CONSTRUCTION

1. Cut 2 felt circles using the 1⅝″ circle pattern (page 104).

2. Place a decorative brad in the center of a circle. Stitch on any other beads and sequins.

3. Place another felt circle on the back of the candy to cover the back of the brad.

4. Embroider around the edges with red perle cotton, using a stitch that goes from front to back over the edge. With the same thread, make a hanging loop, and tie a knot.

Button Tree

MATERIALS

5 green buttons in 5 different sizes for tree

1 yellow button with 2 holes for star

1 brown button with 2 holes for trunk of tree

Red or green perle cotton

2 needles

CONSTRUCTION

1. Cut a 10″ length of perle cotton, and thread each end into a needle.

2. Arrange the buttons in the following order: the brown button, largest to smallest green buttons, then the yellow button.

3. Weave the perle cotton through the holes on the brown button, passing both needles through the same holes, from opposite sides of the button. Tie a knot to hold the button on end (vertical).

4. String the green buttons with the 2 needles going through opposite holes, so the buttons are horizontal. Tie a knot.

5. Weave the yellow button in the same manner as the brown button, and tie a knot to secure.

6. Form a loop with the thread, and tie another knot to make a hanging loop. Trim the tail ends.

Jingle Bell Thread Spools

MATERIALS

Red and green glass beads

Red and green perle cotton

Glue dots

Bells

Wooden spools 1˝ tall

CONSTRUCTION

1. Place 3 glue dots on the wooden spool where the thread would usually go. Position the glue dots so all the horizontal wraps of thread will be anchored by at least 1 dot.

2. Wind the perle cotton thread around the spool, keeping it neat, and tuck in the tail at the glue dots. Cut the thread tail.

3. Cut a length of perle cotton thread. String a bell, the spool, and a bead on the thread.

4. Tie a knot below the bead, form a hanging loop, and tie another knot.

Button Yo-Yo

MATERIALS

Red-and-white fabric for yo-yos: leftover pieces from the tree wallhanging

Red or green embroidery thread

Decorative holiday buttons

CONSTRUCTION

1. Refer to How to Make a Yo-Yo (page 62).

2. Stitch a button to the center of each yo-yo.

3. Make a hanging loop out of embroidery thread.

Count down the days until Halloween with this versatile quilted patchwork calendar. Use a selection of solids for a more modern look, or add in novelty fabrics. Trim down some charm packs for the pocket fronts for a coordinated look. Delete the bottom row to make a Christmas countdown calendar, or change the fabrics for a Thanksgiving theme. The 4˝ pockets are the perfect size for hiding miniature candy bars and other Halloween treats.

Halloween Patchwork

Finished size: 26½˝ × 31½˝ with binding

ARTIST: Elizabeth Hartman

Elizabeth Hartman is a self-taught quiltmaker and pattern designer for modern sewing and quilting. Having grown up in a family that was always making things, she got hooked on quilting as soon as she tried it. She loves the play of color and pattern, the orderliness of the process, and, perhaps best of all, the reward at the end ... a fantastic and functional piece. She is the author of *The Practical Guide to Patchwork*.

EMAIL: elizabeth@ohfransson.com
WEBSITE: ohfransson.com

MATERIALS AND CUTTING

Fabric scraps for pockets:

- Cut 30 pieces 4½˝ × 4˝ of orange print fabrics for the pocket fronts.

- Cut 15 pieces 4½˝ × 9½˝ of yellow print fabrics for the pocket lining.

- Cut 15 pieces 4½˝ × 9½˝ of black print fabrics for the pocket lining.

¼ yard black wool or wool-blend felt for number appliqués

½ yard paper-backed fusible web, such as HeatnBond or Wonder Under

tip

Choose a fusible web based on your construction plans. If you plan to stitch the numbers to the pockets, choose a lightweight fusible web. If you don't want to stitch the numbers, choose a heavyweight, or "no sew," product.

½ yard natural linen or cotton/linen for sashing:

- Cut 9 strips 1½˝ × fabric width.

  Subcut 2 strips into 1 side border piece 1½˝ × 29½˝ and 2 vertical sashing pieces 1½˝ × 4½˝.

  Subcut 2 strips into 1 top/bottom border piece 1½˝ × 26½˝ and 2 vertical sashing pieces 1½˝ × 4½˝.

  Subcut 5 strips into 1 horizontal sashing piece 1½˝ × 24½˝ and 3 vertical sashing pieces 1½˝ × 4½˝.

  From the remaining fabric, cut 1 more vertical sashing piece 1½˝ × 4½˝ (for a total of 24 vertical sashing pieces).

1⅛ yards fabric for backing

2 fabric scraps 4˝ × 4˝ for hanging pockets

31˝ × 36˝ low-loft cotton batting

⅜ yard fabric for binding:

- Cut 4 strips 2½˝ × fabric width; trim away the selvages.

26˝ dowel or piece of balsa wood for hanging

CONSTRUCTION

Note: Use ¼˝ seam allowances unless otherwise noted.

Numbers

For numbers 1–30, you will need the following quantities of each numeral:

0	1	2	3	4	5	6	7	8	9
3	13	13	4	3	3	3	3	3	3

1. Create patterns using a suitable computer font. Pick a font size that prints out about 1¾˝ high. You'll need to reverse the numbers for tracing.

2. Trace the appropriate quantity of each numeral onto the paper side of fusible web. Iron the fusible web with the traced numbers onto the wrong side of wool felt. Carefully cut out the numbers, and, following the manufacturer's instructions, fuse them in the center of the right side of the 4½˝ × 4˝ orange pocket fronts. *Note: The 4½˝ dimension is the width of the pocket.*

3. If desired, stitch around each number using a satin or buttonhole stitch.

Pockets

1. Cut each 4½˝ × 9½˝ piece of black pocket lining fabric into 2 pieces, a 4½˝ × 4˝ piece and a 4½˝ × 4½˝ piece. Pair each set with one of the odd-numbered (1–29) orange pocket fronts.

2. Cut each 4½˝ × 9½˝ piece of yellow pocket lining fabric into 2 pieces 4½˝ × 4˝ and 4½˝ × 4½˝. Pair each set with one of the even-numbered (2–30) orange pocket fronts.

3. Stitch each set of 1 pocket front and 2 yellow or black lining pieces into a finished pocket as follows: Place the orange pocket front and the 4½˝ × 4˝ lining piece together, matching right sides. Stitch the top (above the number) 4½˝ edges together. Press the seam open, and fold in half along the seamline, placing the wrong sides together. Topstitch across the top of the lined pocket front.

4. Place the newly lined pocket front on the right side of the 4½˝ × 4½˝ lining square. (Both the number appliqué and the right side of the lining square should be facing up, and the bottom and side edges should be aligned.) Baste the pieces together, keeping the stitches within about ⅛˝ of the edge. These units will be stitched into the front of the calendar as blocks would be stitched into a quilt top.

Calendar Front

Refer to the assembly diagram (below).

Arrange the pockets in 6 rows of 5. Stitch 1½˝ × 4½˝ pieces of vertical sashing between the pockets in each row, pressing the seams toward the sashing. Stitch the 6 rows together, placing 1½˝ × 24½˝ pieces of horizontal sashing between them. Press. Stitch a 1½˝ × 29½˝ border piece to each side and a 1½˝ × 26½˝ border piece to the top and bottom to complete the calendar top. Press toward the borders as you stitch.

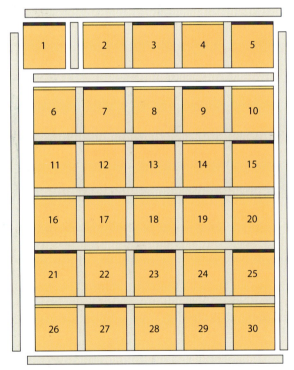

Assembly diagram

Finishing

1. Sandwich the pieced top, batting, and backing as you would if making a quilt. Trim the backing so it is about 4˝ larger than the quilt top on each side. Stitch the layers together by machine quilting the sashing between the pockets (but not over the pockets). After quilting, trim all the layers to match the top, and square up the corners.

2. With wrong sides together, fold each 4˝ hanger square in half diagonally to form a triangle. Place the folded triangles in the top corners, and baste them to the top and side edges of the calendar back, keeping the stitches within about ⅛˝ of the sides.

3. Stitch the binding strips together. Fold lengthwise, and stitch the binding around the edges of the calendar, mitering the corners and catching the hanging pockets and securing them to the back of the calendar.

4. Slide the ends of a dowel or piece of balsa wood into the triangular pockets to hang the finished calendar.

Use upcycled Hawaiian shirts, or have fun buying outlandish fat quarters for this project. Fabric folding and fusible web make a winning combination, and the button embellishments add a realistic touch. This makes a perfect bon voyage gift for a highly anticipated holiday of a lifetime or lets the whole family know it is coming time for a relaxing annual family holiday. Enjoy finding unique embellishments to compliment the chosen fabric theme and display the numbers.

Countdown to Vacation

Finished size: 22˝ × 17˝ with binding

Lynn is a fiber artist, author, and teacher. She has a short attention span, so she loves to try new products and techniques. Her current focus is dyeing and painting on fabric. She is the author of *Fast, Fun & Easy Fabric Dyeing* and *Fast, Fun & Easy Creative Fabric Clocks*.

EMAIL: lynn@lynnkoolish.com
WEBSITES:
lynnkoolish.com
flickr.com/photos/lynnquilter

ARTIST: Lynn Koolish

MATERIALS AND CUTTING

7 rectangles 9½˝ × 10½˝ of Hawaiian shirts or batik fabrics

¾ yards cotton print such as batik

- Cut 1 rectangle 17˝ × 22˝ for the background.
- Cut 1 rectangle 17˝ × 22˝ for the backing.

¼ yard contrasting cotton print

- Cut 2 strips 1˝ × 24˝ for the top and bottom binding.
- Cut 2 strips 1˝ × 19˝ for the side binding.
- Cut 3 strips 2˝ × 6˝ for the hanging tabs.

1 piece 17˝ × 22˝ batting

2⅛ yards paper-backed fusible web

- Cut 7 rectangles 8½˝ × 9½˝ for the shirts.
- Cut 2 strips 1˝ × 22˝ for the top and bottom binding.
- Cut 2 strips 1˝ × 17˝ for the side binding.

7 little flip-flops or other vacation-themed tchotchkes for numbers

25˝ bamboo pole or dowel for hanging

CONSTRUCTION

Shirts

1. Center and iron fusible web to the back of the Hawaiian shirt or batik fabrics. Do not remove the paper backing.

2. On each of the 4 sides, press the ½˝ of fabric not covered by the fusible web over to form a finished edge. Use the edge of the fusible as a guide. Remove the paper backing, and fuse down the 4 edges.

3. With the wrong side facing up, fold in both vertical edges in so they meet in the center. Finger-press.

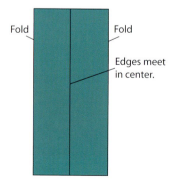

Fold Fold

Edges meet in center.

4. Fold the top horizontal edge to the back, ⅝″ down from the top edge. Finger-press.

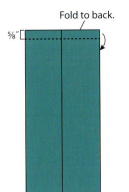

5. Fold the bottom up so its raw edge is ¼″ below the top fold. Finger-press the crease. Unfold. Open out both vertical edges from the bottom to the finger-pressed crease (these will be the sleeves). Finger-press. In the upper part of the unit, keep the vertical edges touching in the center, and fold the outside edges in at an angle so they meet to form the collar. Finger-press.

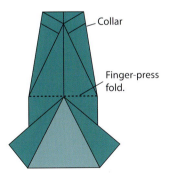

6. Fold up the bottom edge so it tucks under the collar. Finger-press.

7. To finish, fold under the top horizontal edges to form the shoulders. Finger-press.

8. Press the folded shirt using a hot iron. The fusible web will hold the shirt together.

9. Add buttons to the shirt.

Background

1. Layer the backing (wrong side up), batting, and background (right side up).

2. Pin the layers together. Lightly quilt, and stitch around the edges using a scant ¼˝ seam allowance.

3. If desired, cut out motifs or embellishments from fabric, and fuse them to the background.

tip

Iron paper-backed fusible web to the motif fabric, remove the paper backing, and then cut it out.

4. Bind the edges of the project.

5. Arrange the shirts on the background, and pin them in place. Stitch around the outside edges, leaving the top edges open.

6. Add the numbers.

7. Use the 2˝ × 6˝ strips to make hanging loops, and stitch them to the back of your vacation countdown. Add a bamboo pole.

ALOHA!

tip

One of my favorite bindings is a fused binding with a decorative edge. Iron paper-backed fusible web to the binding fabric, remove the paper backing, and cut the strips using a rotary cutter with a decorative blade. Working on top of Silicone Release Paper (by C&T Publishing) or a nonstick appliqué sheet, place strips on opposite sides of the quilt against the quilt top so that half of the binding strip (the long way) is on the quilt top. Press the strips in place. Fold the remaining half of the strips to the back, and press. Trim the short ends of the strips even with the edges of the quilt. The strips for the remaining edges of the quilt should be 1˝ longer than the quilt on each side. Place and press the strips in place as above, wrapping the excess binding ends to the back of the quilt. Topstitch over the binding to make sure it stays in place.

The classic combination of natural linen and white and red embellishment help make this countdown feel at home in any setting. Simple and clean embroidery is used to embellish the pocket fronts, along with some appliqué, buttons, and ribbon. Because each pocket front is embellished with a different design, it is just as fun to make as it is to search out the corresponding date. Add an extra strip of linen at the top or bottom to personalize with a name or special message.

Embroidered Advent Calendar

Finished size: 21˝ × 23˝ with binding

ARTIST: Louise Papas

Louise Papas lives in Melbourne, Australia, with her husband and three young daughters. She enjoys sewing, embroidery, knitting, and crochet and is one-half of the Audrey and Maude design team, creating patterns for quilts, softies, and bags. Louise has had several projects published in various magazines in both Australia and the United Kingdom.

EMAIL: louise.papas@bigpond.com
WEBSITE: lululollylegs.blogspot.com

MATERIALS

¾ yard linen or linen/cotton blend for quilt top and pockets

6 scraps (approximately 4˝ × 4˝) of red patterned fabrics for pockets

¼ yard red homespun for pocket lining

Small scraps of red and white fabrics for appliqué

¾ yard backing fabric

½ yard binding fabric

25˝ × 25˝ square of batting

White and red perle cotton #8 embroidery thread

12˝ of 2 different decorative red-and-white ribbons for pockets 1 and 14

13 white ⅜˝ buttons for pocket 5

9 red ⅜˝ buttons for pocket 7

1 red ½˝ decorative button for pocket 15

CUTTING

Linen or linen/cotton blend

- Cut 1 rectangle 21˝ × 23˝ for the quilt front.
- Cut 18 squares 3¼˝ × 3¼˝ for the pockets.
- Cut 6 squares 3¼˝ × 3¼˝ for the pocket lining.

Red patterned fabrics

- Cut 6 squares 3¼˝ × 3¼˝ for the pockets.

Red homespun

- Cut 18 squares 3¼˝ × 3¼˝ for the pocket lining.

Backing fabric

- Cut 1 square 25˝ × 25˝ for the quilt back.

Binding fabric

- Cut 3 strips 2½˝ × fabric width.
- Cut 1 rectangle 7½˝ × 6˝ for the hanging loops.

CONSTRUCTION

1. Mark the pockets with the appropriate numbers and pictures using an erasable marker.

2. Embroider or appliqué each pocket using the red and white perle cotton threads, ribbons, and buttons. Appliqué patterns are on page 105. Additionally, make a 13/8˝-diameter circle for pocket 13 and 1⅜˝ squares for pockets 6 and 8.

3. Using the red lining on the linen pockets and the linen lining on the red patterned pockets, place the pockets and linings wrong sides together, and stitch across the top only.

4. Position the lined pockets in place on the quilt top. Make sure they are straight, and leave about 1˝ between rows and about ⅝˝ between pockets. Stitch each pocket in place down each side and across the bottom.

5. Embroider "Merry Christmas" on the quilt.

6. Baste the completed front, batting, and back together.

7. Using the red perle cotton thread, hand quilt in between all the pockets horizontally and vertically.

8. Trim the batting and backing even with the quilt top.

9. Make 2 hanging loops as follows: With right sides together, join the short sides of the 7½˝ × 6˝ rectangle, sewing with a ¼˝ seam allowance. Press open, and turn the loop right side out with the seamline running down the middle of the back side. Press.

Cut the loop in half crosswise to make 2 hanging loops 3½˝ × 3˝.

10. Join the 3 binding strips. Bind the quilt, adding the 2 hanging loops into the binding at the top back of the quilt.

You can now place small messages or sweets in the pockets and enjoy the countdown to Christmas.

Birthday Bash

Finished size: 24½″ × 36½″ with binding

Use fun novelty fabric, or select fabrics to compliment a room decor to make up this quilted birthday countdown calendar. Include small gifts or hints as to what the party theme will be to build up excitement to the big day. Construct using grays and blacks and appropriate novelty fabric for an "over the hill" present, and be sure to include humorous reminders of impending old age in the pockets. This design is flexible and fun.

Lisa Penny is an art quilter and textile artist whose work has been featured in several books, galleries, and museum shows. Her work ranges from contemporary twists on traditional quilt styles to art quilts, textile collage, and mixed-media artwork.

EMAIL: Lisa@pennyfabricart.com

WEBSITES:

pennyfabricart.com

facebook.com/PennyFabricArt

ARTIST: Lisa Penny

MATERIALS

⅜ yard birthday fabric 1 for top border and birthday pocket

¼ yard birthday fabric 2 for bottom border

9˝ × 12˝ pieces of 10 assorted novelty fabrics for pockets

1⅜ yards fun print fabric 1 for sashing and backing

¼ yard fun print fabric 2 for side borders and birthday pocket (Can be same as sashing.)

8½˝ × 11˝ rectangle of fun print fabric 3 for numbers (Can be same as sashing.)

26˝ × 38˝ rectangle of fusible batting, such as Hobbs (or plain batting and quilt-basting temporary spray adhesive)

3⅝ yards 1½˝-wide decorative satin ribbon or blanket binding for binding

8½˝ × 11˝ rectangle of paper-backed fusible web (such as Heat*n*Bond UltraHold)

8½˝ × 11˝ rectangle of freezer paper

CUTTING

Birthday fabric 1

- Cut 1 piece 24½˝ × 8½˝ for the top border.
- Cut 1 square 3½˝ × 3½˝ for the birthday pocket.

Birthday fabric 2

- Cut 2 pieces 11˝ × 6½˝ for the bottom border.
- Cut 2 pieces 3½˝ × 1¾˝ for the bottom border.

Assorted novelty fabrics

- Cut 3 squares 3½˝ × 3½˝ from each fabric for the pocket fronts.
- Cut 3 pieces 3½˝ × 4˝ from each fabric for the pocket backs.

Fun print 1

- Cut 36 pieces 1¼˝ × 4˝ for the vertical sashing.
- Cut 7 pieces 20˝ × 1¼˝ for the horizontal sashing.
- Cut 1 piece 26˝ × 38˝ for the backing.

Fun print 2

- Cut 2 pieces 2¾˝ × 26¾˝ for the side borders.
- Cut 1 piece 3½˝ × 4˝ for the birthday pocket back.

CONSTRUCTION

Note: Use ¼˝ seam allowances unless otherwise noted. See note in Numbers (page 82).

Pockets

1. Fold over, press, and stitch a ¼˝ seam at the tops of the 3½˝ × 3½˝ pocket fronts, including the birthday pocket. Press.

2. Position the pocket fronts on top of the pocket backs (right sides facing up), aligning the bottom and side edges. Match up the pairs and placement to get a random look.

3. Referring to the quilt assembly diagram (page 82), arrange and stitch the pockets and vertical sashing strips in rows. Press the seam allowances toward the sashing.

Bottom Border

1. Stitch a 3½˝ × 1¾˝ bottom border piece to the top of the birthday pocket back.

2. Place the birthday pocket front onto the birthday pocket back, aligning the bottom and side edges. Stitch the other 3½˝ × 1¾˝ bottom border piece to the bottom of this unit to close the pocket bottom.

3. Stitch the 11˝ × 6½˝ pieces of the bottom banner to the left and right sides of the birthday pocket unit. Press.

Stitch the Rows and Quilt (in One Step!)

1. Smooth out the batting, and center and baste the backing onto the batting by pressing the wrong side of the backing to the fusible batting or by using the quilt basting spray. Start at the center, and press outward to the edges to get the piece flat and smooth.

2. With the batting side up, measure and mark a dot 19˝ down from the top on the right and left edges. Then very lightly draw a line connecting the dots onto the batting with a pencil. Measure and mark a short vertical line 13˝ in from the left edge to mark the quilt center.

3. Position the Row 3 pocket strip (quilt assembly diagram, page 82) so the bottom edge is ⅛˝ above the horizontal centerline and the middle pocket is centered on the vertical quilt-center mark. Gently smooth the row into place from the center to the edges, using a quilt ruler to keep the bottom edge aligned ⅛˝ above the horizontal centerline. Baste the row down by pressing onto the fusible batting or by using the quilt basting spray.

4. Place a horizontal sashing piece on the bottom edge of Row 3, with right sides together, and pin to hold it in place. Gently roll the bottom of the quilt so it will fit through the machine arm, and stitch the sashing to that bottom edge using a ¼˝ seam allowance, simultaneously stitching the sashing onto the backing and batting. Press toward the sashing,

note

Important: Start the stitching by taking one stitch, raising the presser foot, and pulling the bobbin thread up to the top. Make a couple of tiny backstitches (or fixed stitches if your machine has this capability) to hold the stitching. Also fix the stitch at the end of the row. This attaches the sashing and mimics stitch-in-the-ditch quilting in one step. Because the row piecing is combined with the quilting process, both ends of the row must be fixed so the quilting won't unravel.

5. Referring to the quilt assembly diagram (page 82), repeat Steps 3 and 4 with all the pocket rows and horizontal sashing strips, moving away from the center. Press as you go.

6. Similarly, stitch the left and right side borders to the side edges of the quilt. Press toward the border. Then use this same method to add the bottom border.

Top Border, Quilting, and Hanging Sleeve

1. Measure and mark points on the top border on the left and right edges 4˝ up from the bottom. Make a ½˝ cut at each of those points. Fold and press a ½˝ seam, on each vertical edge, from the point of the cut to the top of the border fabric. Stitch those seams ¼˝ in from the folded edge. Don't worry about the cut edges, as they'll end up hidden inside the binding.

2. Fold, press, and stitch with a ⅜˝ seam allowance along the top edge of the border, using backstitches or fixed stitches at each end to hold the edges.

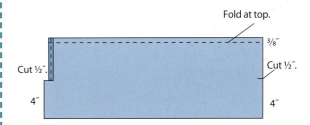

Fold at top.
⅜˝
Cut ½˝.   Cut ½˝.
4˝   4˝

3. Position the bottom edge of the top border along the top edge of the top sashing, right sides together, and stitch the top border onto the top sashing using the same method used to construct the rows (see Stitch the Rows and Quilt, pages 80–81).

4. The top is now completely pieced, with all the horizontal quilting done automatically. Finish the quilting by stitching vertical lines along each column edge. Additional decorative quilting may be used if desired, *but don't stitch over the pockets!*

Quilting in the bottom border can be simple shapes and lines, stipple quilting, or stitching that follows the fabric pattern. *When quilting the top border, leave the big extra flap of fabric up and out of the way, so it isn't quilted down on the back.*

5. When the quilting is finished, trim off any excess batting and backing to square off the quilt. When trimming the top edge, fold back the extra fabric— *do not trim off the top of the fabric!* The top edges of the batting and backing are trimmed so that they align with the spot where the ½˝ cuts from Step 1 (page 81) were made.

6. Fold the fabric flap from the top border over to the back of the quilt. Locate the horizontal stitching line where the top border was stitched onto the top sashing row. The sleeve seam should line up so that it overlaps that line by ¼˝, creating a sleeve. Pin that seam into place (or use a washable acid-free gluestick). Stitch the sleeve into place by stitching in-the-ditch on the front of the quilt in that seamline.

7. Finish the quilt by stitching the 1½˝-wide satin ribbon or blanket binding onto the quilt front, with right sides together and using a ¼˝ seam allowance. Flip the ribbon over to the back, pin it into place, and stitch in-the-ditch on the front along the binding edge so that it catches the ribbon on the back. When stitching the binding on the top edge, pin the sleeve so it remains flat and doesn't twist when stitching. There is enough space on the sides of the sleeve hems so that they won't get caught in the binding.

Numbers

Note: If you prefer to stitch the numbers to the pockets, do so before the pockets are stitched together.

1. Inkjet print, photocopy, or trace numbers from your favorite font onto the paper side of freezer paper. For reference, my numbers are 1¼˝ high.

2. Apply fusible web to the back of the fabric for the numbers. Before removing the fusible paper backing, press the freezer paper with the numbers onto the front of the fabric. Remove the fusible paper backing.

3. Cut out the numbers, and fuse them to the pocket fronts, following the manufacturer's instructions.

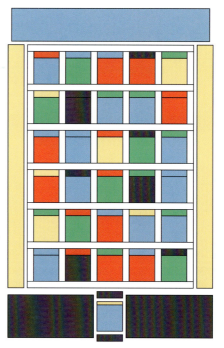

Quilt assembly diagram

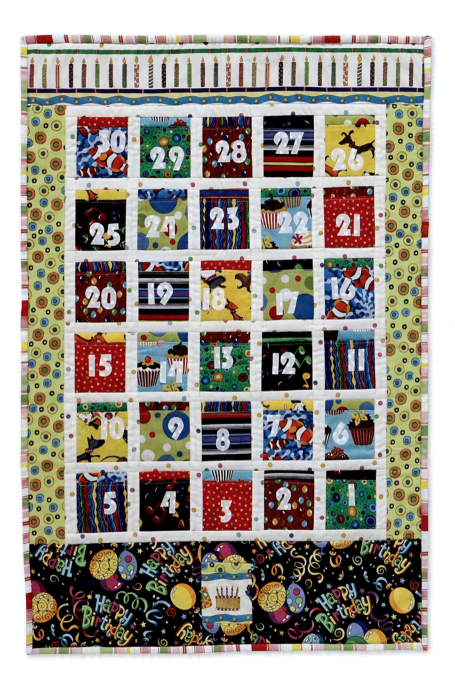

Be My Valentine

Finished size: 20˝ × 19½˝

Use red, black, and white felt to make up this Valentine's Day heart. The scattered pockets with their buttonhole appliquéd numbers can be filled with daily love notes or small pieces of candy. Change the colors and use as a countdown to an anniversary or give as a gift to the organizer of a special event you are participating in. Use buttons to embellish if the calendar is being used for a child older than three; otherwise leave them off to avoid a potential choking hazard.

ARTIST: Wendy Sloneker

Omni Artist and cowgirl-at-heart, Wendy Sloneker has designed and produced myriad garments, accessories, and home decorations in varieties of media. She has taught art and creativity classes for more than fifteen years. Recent experience includes screening, producing, selling, and promoting at Seattle's Pike Place Market. She coaches and encourages folks to show up and try the things they are curious about ... and even scared of. She was a contributor to Jennifer Worick's *The Prairie Girl's Guide to Life*, Jane Davila and Elin Waterston's *Art Quilt Workbook*, Art with Heart's *Chill & Spill: Educator's Companion* and *Chill & Spill: Therapist's Companion*. Additional original craft content pieces appeared on craftstylish.com.

EMAIL: friendywendy@yahoo.com

WEBSITE: wendysloneker.com

MATERIALS

⅝ **yard red felt**

4–6 squares 9˝ × 12˝ each of black and white felt *or* ¼ yard each

Red, black, and white embroidery floss

Embellishments, such as buttons, decorative brads, beads, sequins, or spangles

⅛˝-diameter dowel, 12˝ long

Fabric glue

CUTTING

White felt

- Cut 7 rectangles 3¼˝ × 4˝.
- Cut 20 squares 1¼˝ × 1¼˝.

Freehand cut or use your favorite pattern to cut out numbers 1–7.

tip

For freehand cutting, start with 7 rectangles of white felt measuring 2½˝ × 2¾˝. Cut the numbers by using as much of the rectangle as possible, and they will fit beautifully on the black rectangles.

Black felt

- Cut 7 rectangles 2¾˝ × 3˝.
- Cut 21 squares 1¼˝ × 1¼˝.

Red felt

Fold the red felt in half, with the fold at the top and the opening at the bottom of your workspace. Be sure to keep the fold intact so the dowel will hang in the fold at the top of the heart shape. Cut the heart shape freehand, or make a pattern. You will have a front piece and a back piece held together by the folds at the top.

CONSTRUCTION

1. Thread a double length of red embroidery floss in a needle, and knot the 2 ends together.

2. Using a blanket stitch, or any of your favorite decorative stitches, outline and attach each of the white felt numbers onto a black felt rectangle. Keep the knots at the back of your work.

3. When the black rectangles are completed, adhere them onto the white rectangles with fabric glue. Let them dry completely.

tip

Stitch the numbered pockets and embellishments on just the front of the heart shape; don't stitch through to the back layer.

4. Unfold the red heart shape, and place it flat on the table.

5. Arrange the white rectangle units on the front of the red heart shape. Pat them lightly to set them in place, and pin them to the red felt.

6. Thread a double length of black embroidery floss in a needle, and knot the 2 ends together. Blanket stitch the 2 sides and bottom of the white rectangles into place on the red felt. Leave the top side unstitched so you can slip goodies into this pocket later.

7. Scatter a small handful of buttons across the front of the heart shape, and stitch them into place where they land.

8. Fold the red felt back into the heart shape. Place the 1¼˝ squares along the outside edges of the heart between the 2 layers, so they protrude from the edge.

9. Thread a double length of black embroidery floss in a needle, and knot the 2 ends together. Beginning ½˝ from the top fold of the red heart shape, and using a simple running stitch, stitch the 2 layers of the heart shape together, with the black and white checks sandwiched in between the red layers. Sew ½˝-long stitches around the heart shape, checking every few inches to make sure you are stitching through all the layers. Remember to leave ½˝ of space from the top of the fold so you can slip the dowel inside later.

10. Slip the dowel into place, hang, and fill!

What's not to love about this happy row of Santas? Have fun collecting a dozen fat quarters to make these twelve pockets. This project is perfect for those looking for a shorter countdown to Christmas. Hang them across the mantel, and you have a decorative garland as well as a whimsical and unique calendar. Add a bell to the bottom if the calendar is being used for a child older than three; otherwise leave them off to avoid a potential choking hazard.

Santa Pennie Pockets

Finished size: 6½″ × 11″

ARTIST: Monica Solorio-Snow

Born and raised in Walnut Creek, California, Monica was never more than a few minutes from one of the best shopping meccas in the world. Wallet permitting, anything and everything was at her fingertips. In the 1990s, she moved to Astoria, Oregon—a small town on the northern coast, about a 90-minute drive to the "The Big City" (Portland). After searching high and low in Portland for a cute fix for something, she realized it was much easier to sew something than to spend an entire day driving around looking for it. She found that making something rather than buying something was empowering and satisfying ... and much more fun! Sewing and making is her "happy," and she hopes to share some of that joy with others.

WEBSITES:

thehappyzombie.com   twitter.com/Happy_Zombie

MATERIALS

12 fat quarters total of red, pink, and aqua

½ yard white wool felt (35% wool / 65% rayon blend preferred)

Embroidery floss in red, pink, and aqua

12 jingle bells

20˝ × 20˝ HeatnBond Lite (for Santa hats)

CUTTING

See the patterns on page 102. Note: Cut felt, fabric, and fusible hats about ¼˝ larger all around than the pattern, and trim them to size after pressing for a crisp, sealed fused edge.

Fat quarters

- Cut 1 square 12˝ × 12˝ from each fat quarter, and then cut each square diagonally for a total of 24 triangles for the inner and outer pockets.

- Cut 12 hats.

White felt

- Cut 12 faces and 12 hats.

Fusible web

- Cut 12 hats.

CONSTRUCTION

Hats and Faces

1. Following the manufacturer's directions, fuse each cotton hat to a felt hat, wrong sides together.

2. Blanket stitch around the sides of the fused hats and around the beards. Embroider the face details; satin stitch the centers of the eyes, using the pattern (page 102) for placement. Use a backstitch to outline the faces and numbers 1–12.

Pennie Pocket

1. Layer an outer pocket triangle right side up, the Santa face right side up (centered on the long diagonal leg of the outer pocket triangle, and with raw edges aligned), the hat right side down (centered over the Santa face with raw edges aligned), and then the inner pocket triangle, right side down, on top of the stack. Stitch along the diagonal leg using a ¼˝ seam allowance.

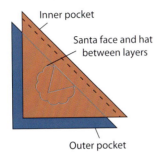

Inner pocket

Santa face and hat between layers

Outer pocket

2. Press the seam allowances open.

3. Fold the piece diagonally, perpendicular to the previously sewn seam and with right sides together. Stitch with a ¼˝ seam allowance around 2 edges, stopping ¾˝ past the corner. Leave a 4˝ opening for turning, and continue stitching.

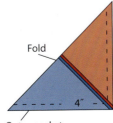

Fold

4˝

Outer pocket

4. Turn right side out. Topstitch over the opening, stitching as close as possible to the outer fabric's opening. *Note: This edge will not show when the Santa pennie is complete.*

5. Turn over and tuck the inner pocket fabric to the inside of the pocket so that the wrong sides of the inner and outer pockets are against each other. Twist the pocket so the inner seam is centered. A diamond shape is formed, and the top point forms the back flap when it's turned over onto itself. Press.

Back of pennie pocket

6. Stitch a jingle bell to the bottom of the Santa pennie.

7. Attach a snap or hook-and-loop dots to secure the back flap onto itself to make a tube for running ribbon, rickrack, or garland through. If the back side won't be visible, a simple straight pin or tack stitch will work nicely too.

8. Repeat Steps 1–7 to make 12 Santa pennie pockets.

9. String the Santa pennie pockets together to form a countdown garland. Fill each pocket with treats.

Celebrate

Finished size: 12˝ × 43˝ with binding

This banner holds seven substantial pockets to celebrate the week before a special event. With a lot of room to customize and add embellishments, this is a flexible design that can be used to house gifts or messages. Buttonhole stitching adds a casual feel, as does the use of the canvas duck fabric.

ARTIST: Sweetwater

Sweetwater is a family-run design company located in northeastern Colorado. Sweetwater is actually a spinoff of its parent company, Farmyard Creations, which began as a quilt company in 1985, providing quilt patterns and designing fabrics for quilt stores. In 2001, Sweetwater was launched by taking the fabric designs of Farmyard Creations and turning them into paper. Coordinating stickers and other accessories were then added to give the Sweetwater line a soft, sophisticated style. Recently, Sweetwater has been focusing its energy on fresh and innovative graphic design, as well as a fun line of fabric and quilt patterns.

EMAIL: info@sweetwaterstreet.com

WEBSITE: sweetwaterstreet.com

MATERIALS AND CUTTING

½ yard 54˝-wide canvas duck

- Cut 1 rectangle 12˝ × 43˝ for the background.
- Cut 7 outside pocket pieces using the pattern (page 106).

¼ yard each of 7 prints for the pocket lining, numbers, and letters

½ yard fabric for backing (at least 44˝ wide, or piece as needed)

½ yard batting (at least 44˝ wide)

⅜ yard fabric for binding

- Cut 4 strips, 2½˝ × fabric width.

8 buttons, 1˝ diameter

½˝-diameter wooden dowel, 14˝ long

Dark brown embroidery floss (DMC #3790)

½ yard paper-backed fusible web

CONSTRUCTION

Note: Use ¼˝ seam allowances.

Appliqué

1. Freehand draw or use your favorite font to make letters about 2¾˝ tall to spell "CELEBRATE" and the numbers 1–7 approximately 4˝ tall to fit on the front of the pockets. Reverse the letters and numbers, and trace them onto the paper side of the fusible web. Roughly cut them out.

2. Following the manufacturer's directions, iron the cut fusible web pieces to the wrong side of 7 printed pieces of fabric.

3. Cut out the letters and numbers on the traced lines.

4. Peel off the paper backing, and iron the numbers to the canvas front pocket pieces, placing each number in a different position on the pocket (refer to

the project photo, page 93). Be sure to allow space for the seam allowance on the pocket.

5. Iron the word "CELEBRATE" to the canvas background, positioning the letters 2½˝ from the left edge.

6. With 3 strands of embroidery floss, stitch a blanket stitch around each number and letter.

Pockets

1. From the same fabric that was used for the number appliqué, cut 3 pieces 5˝ × 6˝.

2. With right sides together, place a fabric piece over a canvas pocket piece.

3. Trim the top edge of the fabric to match the curve on the canvas.

4. Stitch on the curved edge, clip the seam, and turn over the fabric to the back of the canvas pocket piece; press. Treat the fabric and canvas as a single piece.

5. With right sides together, place the canvas pocket piece (with the appliquéd number) between the remaining 5˝ × 6˝ fabric pieces, aligning the bottom and side edges.

6. Stitch around the rectangle, leaving a 2˝ opening at the bottom. Trim the corners of the rectangle, and turn the piece right side out through the 2˝ opening at the bottom. Press the rectangle.

7. Topstitch close to the edges of all 4 sides

8. Repeat Steps 1–7 for the remaining pockets.

Finishing

1. Cut the batting and backing slightly larger than the front of the banner.

2. Layer the top, batting, and backing together, and pin or baste in place.

3. Position the pockets vertically on the canvas background, 2˝ from the right edge and ½˝ apart from each other.

4. Topstitch ¼˝ from the edge of each pocket, stitching through all the layers.

5. Trim the backing and batting even with the quilt top.

6. Piece and stitch together the binding strips to make one long strip.

7. Fold the binding in half lengthwise, and stitch the binding to the edges of the banner.

8. Stitch the 8 buttons in the empty space to the left of the pockets, scattering them 3˝–4˝ apart.

9. Cut a strip of fabric 1¾˝ × fabric width. Fold the long raw edges toward the center of the strip, and press. Fold in half lengthwise with the folded edges together, and press. Topstitch close to the long edge of the strip on both sides.

10. Cut the strip into 3 pieces 12˝ long.

11. Fold each strip in half crosswise, and stitch the folded edge to the back of the banner next to the binding at the top, placing one at each side and one in the center.

12. Tie the banner around the wooden dowel.

Welcome Home Coasters

Finished wallhanging size: approximately 6½˝ × 33˝
Finished coaster size: approximately 5˝ × 4˝

Use raw-edge appliqué to create this pretty and practical countdown to moving into a new home. Start from the top with the numbers facing front, and turn each around in the week before the move. But this calendar is more than decorative —each of the five individual squares detach to become coasters! Hang on your wall, and you have handy access to them for all the last-minute well-wishers who stop by. Once the move is complete, hang this banner with the numbers to the back for a decorative reminder of new beginnings and happy tidings.

ARTIST: Laurraine Yuyama

Laurraine is a self-taught quilter who creates all her own designs and patterns. She has fun combining elements from her dual passions of patchwork and pottery—creating dishes with patches of intricate patterns, and quilting three-dimensional teapots and teacups. She is greatly inspired by tea, Japanese country patchwork, and the online craft community, where she is known as PatchworkPottery. She sews, blogs, and sells her pattern booklets online from her bright attic studio in Vancouver, British Columbia, Canada.

EMAIL: laurraine@patchworkpottery.com
WEBSITE: patchworkpottery.com

MATERIALS AND CUTTING

See the patterns on pages 107–111.

¼ yard natural linen

- Cut 1 roof shape.
- Cut 1 rectangle 7˝ × 3˝ for the welcome mat.
- Cut 7 rectangles 5¾˝ × 4¾˝ for the coasters.

12˝ × 10˝ piece of striped natural linen

- Cut 1 roof shape.
- Cut 1 rectangle 7˝ × 3˝ for the welcome mat.
- Cut 1 rectangle 5¾˝ × 4¾˝ for the coaster.

7˝ × 10˝ piece of print natural linen

- Cut 2 rectangles 5¾˝ × 4¾˝ for the coasters.

16˝ × 20˝ piece of batting

- Cut 1 rectangle 6½˝ × 8˝ for the roof.
- Cut 1 rectangle 3½˝ × 3˝ for the bird.
- Cut 1 rectangle 8˝ × 4˝ for the welcome mat.
- Cut 5 rectangles 6½˝ × 5½˝ for the coasters.

10˝ × 12˝ piece of Lite Steam-A-Seam 2 or similar double-sided iron-on fusible web

Fabric scraps with various patterns and colors for appliqué

2½˝ × 11½˝ piece of dark brown and black check for roof binding

5˝ × 3˝ piece of teal print

- Cut 2 rectangles 2½˝ × 3˝ for the bird.

9˝ piece of ½˝-wide ribbon for hanging loop

4 buttons, ½˝–¾˝ diameter, in a variety of colors and shapes

5 buttons, ⅛˝ diameter

12 beige buttons, ⅜˝ diameter

Tiny scrap of brown felt for beak

Embroidery floss in dark brown and beige

Embroidery needle and another needle with large eye

Water-erasable fabric pen

CONSTRUCTION

Coasters, Welcome Mat, and Roof

1. Referring to the photos (page 98) and the patterns (pages 107–111), tape the patterns to a light source, such as a lightbox or a window. One by one, place the linen fabrics over the base patterns, and trace the corresponding patterns onto the various linen rectangles with a water-erasable fabric pen. Repeat for each linen rectangle, centering and tracing each appliqué and number pattern, and marking button and loop placement.

2. Using a pencil, trace all the appliqué shapes onto the first backing sheet of the double-sided fusible web, adding overlap where needed. Turn the web sheet over, and darken the traced lines on the second backing sheet. Remove the first backing sheet, and iron the fusible web onto the back of the fabric scraps. Cut out the pieces on the lines.

3. Peel off the remaining backing paper, and position each appliqué piece on the coaster, starting with the appliqué background. Overlap the shapes as you work your way to the foreground, using the traced image on the linen as a guide.

4. Place the linen rectangles with the appliqué windows and doors on a batting rectangle, right side up. Topstitch the raw edges of the shapes through the batting as well as the linen layer. I also used a machine blanket stitch. Topstitch the appliqué numbers through the linen layer only.

5. Using a backstitch and 6 strands of dark brown floss, embroider the lettering and remaining traced lines through the linen layer backed with batting.

6. Pair up a front and a back for the roof, coasters, and welcome mat as follows:

Front image with background	Back number (on plain linen background)
Welcome mat (striped linen)	1
Door (print linen)	2
Curtain (plain linen)	3
Flowers (striped linen)	4
Shade (plain linen)	5
Arch window (print linen)	6
Roof (striped linen)	7

7. Place each pair of fronts and backs right sides together, and stitch along the edges, rounding the corners and leaving a 3″ opening on one side. For the roof, leave the top edge unstitched.

8. Clip the corners, trim the seam allowances, and turn the units right side out. Stitch the openings closed using a blind stitch.

9. Topstitch ³⁄₁₆˝ in from the outer edge of each unit, including the top edge of the roof.

Roof

1. Fold the 2½˝ × 11½˝ strip ¼˝ under at the short ends. Press. Fold the strip in half lengthwise, wrong sides together, and press. Open, and fold the long raw edges to the center crease, and press again.

2. Find the center of the strip, and line it up with the point of the roof. Cover the top edge of the roof with the strip, and pin it in place. Miter the peak as needed. Stitch ⅛˝ in from the edge of the strip along the entire length.

3. Fold the hanging ribbon in half, and tack it securely in place on the embroidered side of the roof.

4. Trace the bird shape (pattern, page 110) onto the wrong side of a 2½˝ × 3˝ teal rectangle. Place the second teal rectangle on top, with right sides together, and then add a layer of batting. Insert the felt beak facing in toward the center, and stitch directly on the traced line, leaving an opening at the tummy. Clip the corners, notch the curves, trim the seam allowances, and turn the bird right side out. Stitch the opening closed using a blind stitch. Using brown floss, add a running stitch for the wing and a French knot for the eye.

5. Position the bird over the tip of the roof, covering the ends of the ribbon, and whipstitch it in place.

Buttons and Loops

1. Attach all the decorative buttons, being careful not to stitch through to the other side. Attach the beige hanging buttons through all the layers, using beige embroidery floss.

2. Cut 12 pieces 4¼˝ long of beige embroidery floss, and knot the ends to form loops.

3. Attach the loops, threading them through the coasters as marked.

tip

Poking holes in the coaster before pulling the loops through makes the job easier.

Patterns

BACK TO SCHOOL

Project on page 7.

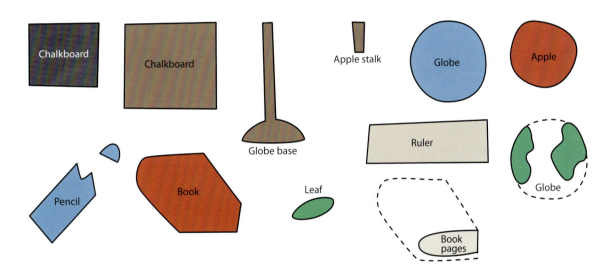

Chalkboard

Chalkboard

Apple stalk

Globe

Apple

Globe base

Ruler

Globe

Pencil

Book

Leaf

Book pages

SANTA'S SLIPPERS

Project on page 10.

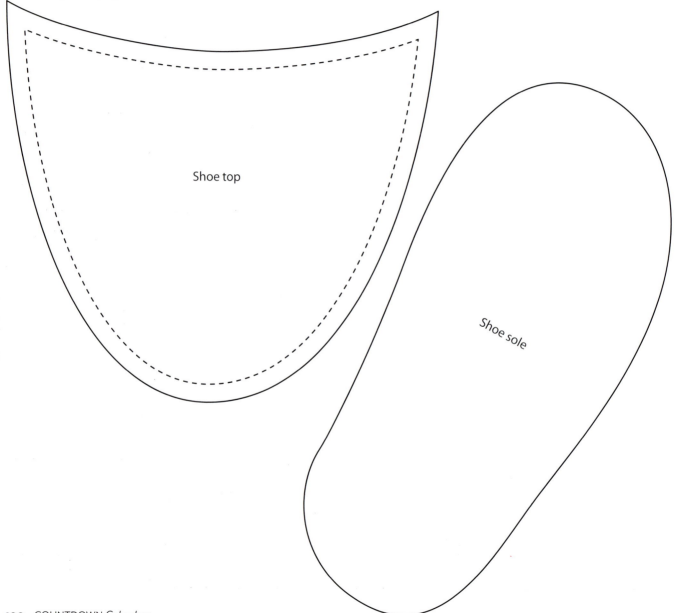

Shoe top

Shoe sole

EIGHT DAYS OF HANUKKAH

Project on page 28.

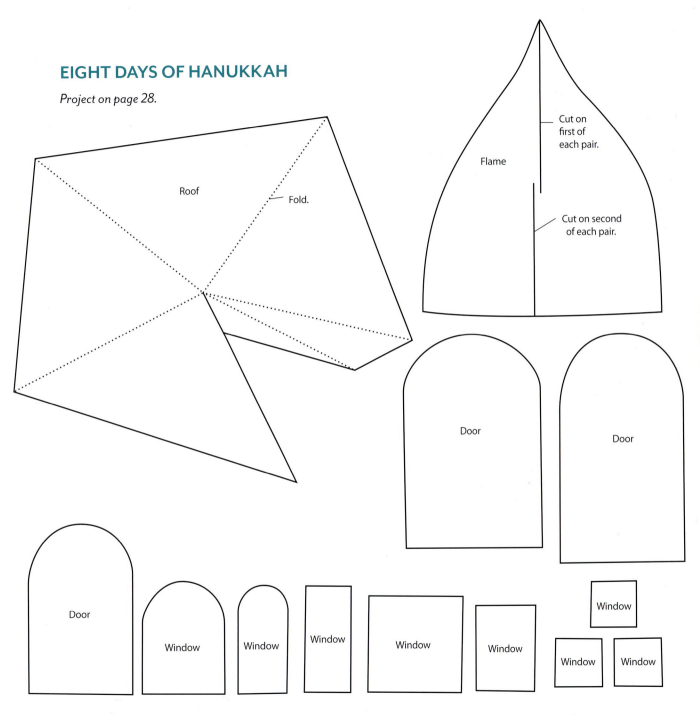

Roof

Fold.

Flame

Cut on first of each pair.

Cut on second of each pair.

Door

Door

Door

Window

Window

Window

Window

Window

Window

Window

Window

WEDDING DAY POCKETS

Project on page 53.

SANTA PENNIE POCKETS

Project on page 87.

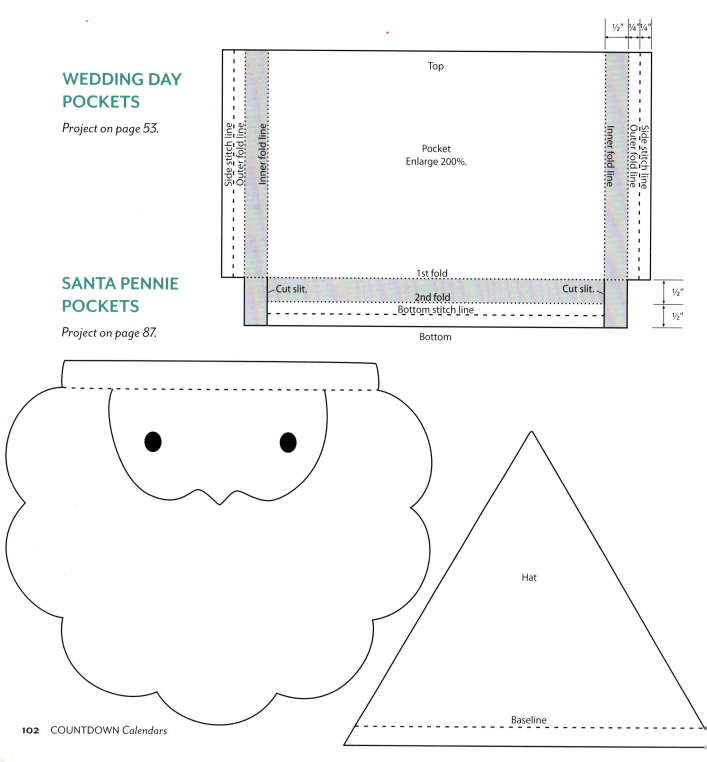

½" ¼" ¼"

Top

Side stitch line
Outer fold line
Inner fold line

Pocket
Enlarge 200%.

Inner fold line
Outer fold line
Side stitch line

1st fold

Cut slit.
2nd fold
Cut slit.

Bottom stitch line

½"
½"

Bottom

Hat

Baseline

YOU'VE BEEN FRAMED

Project on page 50.

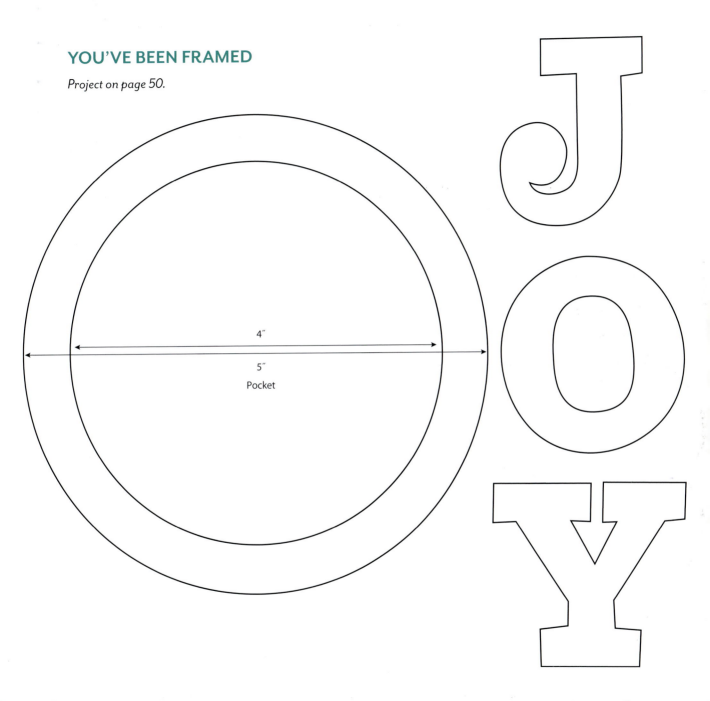

4"

5"
Pocket

YO-YO ADVENT TREE

Project on page 60.

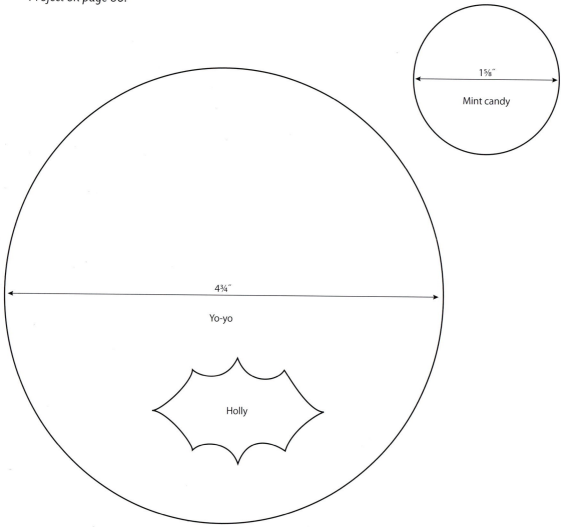

1⅝″

Mint candy

4¾″

Yo-yo

Holly

EMBROIDERED ADVENT CALENDAR

Project on page 75.

CELEBRATE

Project on page 90.

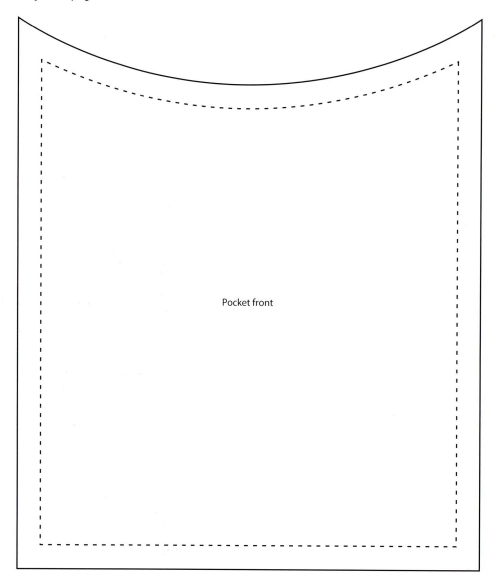

Pocket front

BIRTHDAY CAKE COUNTDOWN

Project on page 40.

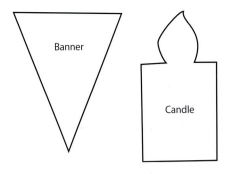

WELCOME HOME COASTERS

Project on page 94.

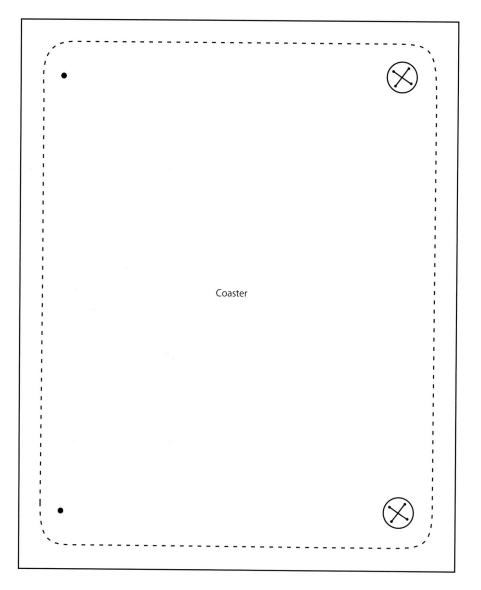

Coaster

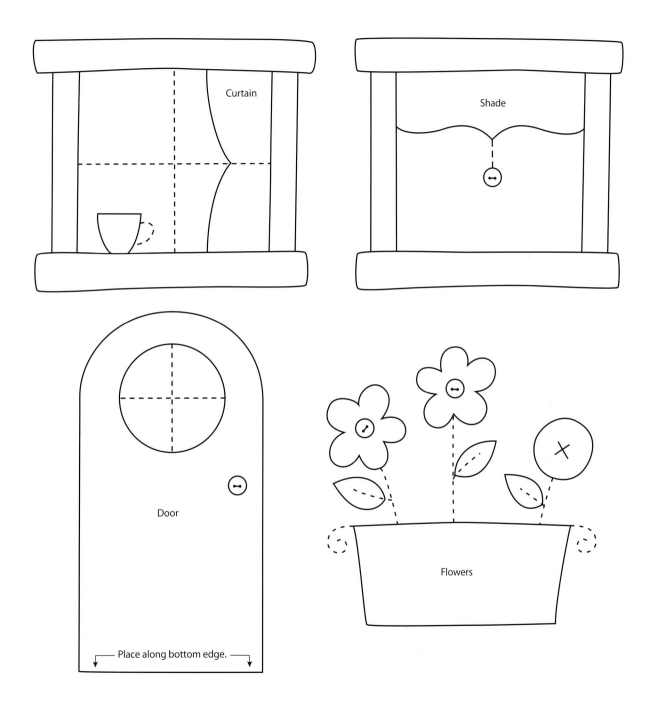

Curtain

Shade

Door

Place along bottom edge.

Flowers

WELCOME HOME COASTERS *(continued)*

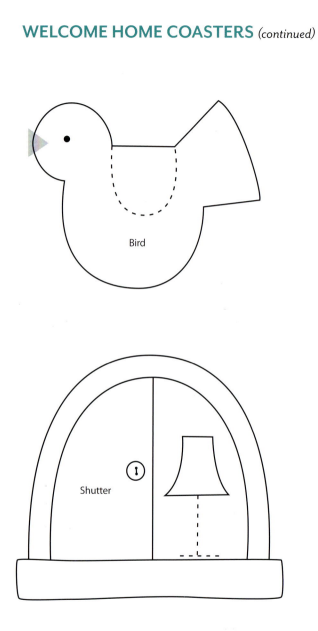

Bird

Shutter

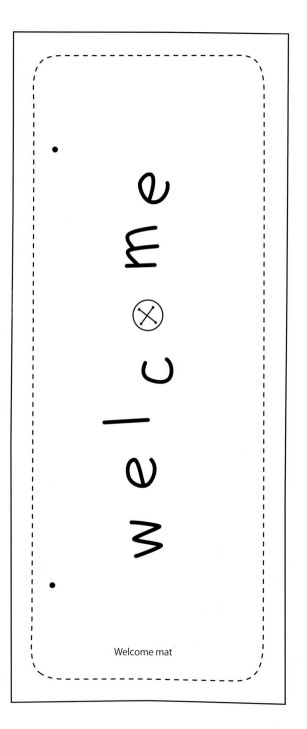

welcome

Welcome mat

Roof

home
sweet
home

stash BOOKS

fabric arts for a handmade lifestyle

If you're craving beautiful authenticity in a time of mass-production...Stash Books is for you. Stash Books is a line of how-to books celebrating fabric arts for a handmade lifestyle. Backed by C&T Publishing's solid reputation for quality, Stash Books will inspire you with contemporary designs, clear and simple instructions, and engaging photography.

www.stashbooks.com